Hire to Inspire

What Great Leaders Do
to Consistently Achieve *Winning* Results

by Yolanda Mangrum, DDS, and Jennifer Chevalier

ISBN-13: 9781505521047
ISBN-10: 1505521041

"Hiring the right team member is not as much a science as it is an art. This book provides key tools and invaluable golden nuggets that allow great entrepreneurs to achieve not only massive business growth but personal satisfaction and happiness. I would recommend this book without hesitation to all of our law firm clients."

- Ali Oromchian, JD, LL.M., Dental & Medical Counsel, PC
www. HRforHealth.com

"Make your next hire your best hire. One of the biggest challenges for most employers is finding the right people for their business. Yolanda and Jennifer have provided a wonderful volume of extremely necessary examples and direction to help achieve the best results in the hiring process. Inspiring, easy to apply solutions and input from leaders in our profession."

- Virginia Moore, Motivational Speaker, Author and
Consultant Moore Practice Success, www.virginiamoore.com

"Bravo for writing a book that details the dental profession's business pearls of success, by the experts of the profession. This book is a no nonsense toolkit that will continue to teach team members how to be an asset to the team and accountable to the practice."

- Bete Johnson, Vice President of Business Development in Banking

"This is unlike any other book I have ever read in its category. After twenty years of practicing in my field working with many employees, hiring, mentoring, and inspiring creative work, great productivity and continuously try to inspire to be the best, *Hire to Inspire* changed the way I think about how to approach my way of work. This well-written book offers the best road map for wannabe leaders to become real leaders and effectively lead and be able to see the best results ever imagined."

- Mohsen Ghoreishi, Architect & CEO/President of Kohan,
www.kohaninc.com

"We have 125 employees and sometimes we have a high turnover rate. The way to overcome those times is to get back to basics and look at your culture and core beliefs. This book is a great blueprint on where and how to start. This is required reading for my management team."

- Robert Martino, DDS, CEO, Wilmar Management

"Using the exact skills described in this book, and empowering my wonderful dental team to share and mold our practice's vision, I was able to retire 10 years early from practice, enjoy a balanced and rich life, while my wonderful team moved on to highly successful careers in the healthcare field. Dr. Yolanda and Jennifer hit the nail on the head by interviewing the best coaches in communication, goal setting, organizational behavior, and leadership and sharing their important findings with you. If you read and apply the messages here, you will tap your full potential as a leader, dentist, and human being. A must-read for anyone wanting to succeed in their journey."

- Ronald Yee, D.D.S., Professor, Consultant, Retired Dentist

We dedicate this book to the loves of our lives, our husbands (Yolanda's husband Thomas Walsh and Jennifer's husband Andre Chevalier) whom we would walk through hot coals for. You are our dear friends, patient partners and solid rocks to anchor us down when we float away. It's your unlimited devotion, understanding and support that made all this possible.

We also dedicate this book to our children, who continually inspire us to become better people and give us our power of purpose. We will always be there to lift you up, dust you off and point you in the right direction.

Love you guys to the moon and back,
Yolanda and Jennifer

CONTENTS

Foreword   i

Introduction and Acknowledgements   iv

Chapter 1:   Positive "I Can" Self-Talk: A Conversation with Steven Campbell   1

Chapter 2:   Being the Role Model - The Leadership Characteristics   7
Of Excellence: A Conversation with Lois Banta,
Rhonda Savage and Linda Miles

Chapter 3:   Telling the Story of Why and Having a Clear Vision: 21
A Conversation with Fred Joyal

Chapter 4:   Core Values - Lead By Example: Conversations with   31
Joseph Stith and Bob Leonard

Chapter 5:   Who to Hire, Inspire or Fire, from the Employee Perspective: 41
Conversations with Tonya Lanthier and Desiree Guevara

Chapter 6:   Impeccable Communication: It's Always Showtime: 53

A Conversation with Michael Allosso

Chapter 7:   Embracing Change for Growth - C.A.N.I.®6:   63
A Conversation with Shannon Richkowski

Chapter 8:   Developing Talent through Mentoring, Praise and   71
Encouragement: A Conversation with Vicki McManus

Chapter 9:   Culture of Accountability: A Conversation with Vicki Suiter   85

Chapter 10:   Participatory Ownership: A Conversation with Bernie Stoltz   93

Chapter 11:   Unstoppable Teams Go Further: by Jennifer Chevalier   101

Conclusion: Success is a Journey, Not a Destination: 107
Yolanda Mangrum DDS

Appendix I: Leadership Test   112

Appendix II: Organization Culture Test   114

Appendix III: A, B, C-level Employee Test   116

Appendix IV: 1:1 Growth Conference Worksheet   118

Appendix V: Happiness Assessment   119

Endnotes and Recommended Resources   120

Foreword

Because I work with business owners, I often hear, "Why don't my employees just do what they're supposed to do?" "There's no accountability!" or, "All they really want is a paycheck." The business owner often sees employees as his biggest stressor.

What would it be like if each employee was a true team member, aligned with your vision, taking "ownership" in your business, and supporting you in reaching your goals?

As a co-founder of Fortune Management, I continuously study what makes businesses grow and prosper. One of the fundamentals is great leadership. Many valuable books and seminars teach the characteristics of great leadership and management. You can find many pearls of wisdom in these books and seminars. The bottom line is that it all boils down to the language we repeatedly say to ourselves. And that comes from the meanings we have given to events that we experienced, often when we were young. These become our belief systems, the paradigms we operate from, and the mindsets we think from. Even though these can change slightly as we grow older, it usually takes an "aha" moment to cause a paradigm shift or a massive change.

Albert Einstein said, "The significant problems that we face cannot be solved at the same level of thinking we were at when we created them." Even though I know this is true, I so often find myself trying to power through the challenge rather than clarify my thinking about the challenge! What result might be possible if I changed my thinking to knowing I can solve this problem easily or better, that I know that my team can solve this easily or better if I create an environment that allows them to contribute and to be accountable for the solution?

I have seen mediocre employees turn into outstanding team members when the work environment is supportive. The leader's belief in each team member's desire to grow and contribute is the foundation. Having a vision and having the leader's expectations clearly defined, then having the team design and agree on codes of conduct and core values will create this environment. Still, they may not immediately turn into a great team. So the leader's next step is to elegantly hold each team member accountable, support them, and celebrate wins. When an outstanding environment and accountabilities are put into place, employees either step up to the plate, or leave.

In business, being a great leader and having a great team that rallies behind your vision and purpose as if it was their own creates remarkable results.

So how do we become great leaders? What mindset is the employer operating from on a regular basis? Is he thinking, "I'm just not a good leader"? Is she thinking, "That's just not me"? We attribute leadership to some sort of talent or innate ability. Fortunately, leadership is not an innate ability; it can be learned. And if we learn the belief systems and thinking of great leaders, we too will become great leaders.

There are many types of leadership styles: the laissez-faire approach, the collaborative team approach, the authoritarian approach, and the transformational approach, to name a few. If you think you aren't a leader, you are communicating this. Remember, you cannot *not* communicate. Your *not leading* is actually leading your team to *not be aligned with* your vision and your purpose. No one style is the best; no one style works in all situations. In leading my own teams, I have used all styles. However, I know that I'm using them deliberately to fulfill our vision. Unexamined, we are just using one style and might not be getting our desired outcomes. As you read this book, you will be able to see what styles will give you the results you want.

While you are discovering (and remembering) the distinctions in the book that make great leaders, I will tell you a few things I did to become the leader I am today. First, do you have a vision that inspires you? Get yourself totally connected to your vision every single morning; that will make your thinking consistent with your vision. If your mind focuses on what's wrong, immediately shift your thinking back to your vision. To create an environment in your office that will make your team extraordinary, be the emotional state you want to see from your team. Share your vision and then create it. Let them know how you are going to support that vision. How can they help fulfill it? Honor their contribution and ideas, and ask how you can support them. When people are inspired, they create amazing goals. Have them be accountable to those goals, guiding them toward who they will become by attaining those goals.

I wish that was all there was to it....

Again, our results come from our actions, which come from the mindset we choose on a regular basis. Our mindsets (again, what we are thinking at any given moment) are totally shaped by the meanings we give what is happening around us, provided by our belief systems. Most times, we do not recognize the mindset we are in. Even though I was working on becoming a great leader, unless I was conscious of it, I would revert back to the old way of thinking. I resolved to change and at one time, had reminders on my Day-Timer. Now, reminders asking, "Where am I thinking from?" pop up in my iPhone throughout the day!

What if we stopped and asked ourselves on a regular basis, "What outcomes are we getting? Are they a match for our vision and goals? What mindset would I need right now to lead my team to achieve those outcomes? What mindset would my team have to have to achieve those outcomes?"

My definition of being a powerful leader is having the ability to consistently create your vision and purpose and the outcomes that support that vision or purpose, and to influence your team to be so aligned with you that they consistently create your vision, purpose, and outcomes, taking them on as their own.

The goal of this book is to help you distinguish the mindsets that would make you effective in fulfilling your purpose, your vision, and your goals. My wish is for you to achieve your dreams, and to have a team so aligned with you that all your goals are reached!

René Schubert

René Schubert is a Partner and Director of Fortune Management. For the past 30 years, she has been a perpetual student of personal growth and development, with a specific focus on team building and motivation. René, with Dr. McLeod and Dr. Bass, works closely with Anthony Robbins in the development and delivery of management and team building seminars throughout the United States and Canada. She has presented over 1,000 seminars, workshops, and training programs spanning a period of over 20 years, and has positively impacted thousands of people with her work.

Introduction and Acknowledgments

Hire to Inspire is a collaborative result of having received generous insight from incredible mentors who are experts in their field on what it takes to hire, inspire and lead a team to achieve winning results. The goal of this book is to support leaders in creating an organization of leaders leading leaders, where individual employees are so passionate about contributing to their work that they see themselves as being in partnership with their employer.

I set out on the journey of writing this book to directly benefit my own team's understanding of what I mean by, "I want to be surrounded only by happy people who see themselves as partners in our organization." Yes, this may sound like I am in search of Camelot or some fairytale work environment, but it is how I believe we can each find our happiness and power of purpose. According to a 2010 Gallup poll,[1] employee disengagement was at an all-time high; seventy percent of all American workers said they were unhappy at work. This is seriously concerning, given that many of us spend more time at work than anywhere else. Why not find work that is meaningful, so that our talents can be utilized, giving us a power of purpose and a sense of accomplishment?

I can tell you after nearly twenty years of being an employer and a leader to hundreds of employees, there is no such thing as a perfect leader or a perfect employee. We are all well intended human beings doing the best we can and, hopefully, learning from our mistakes along the way. I will admit it would take another book to explain all the "failures that led to my successes," and I know it has been through the worst moments of my life that I have gained the most character, courage and strength for the future.

With that being said, I would like to acknowledge every one of my past and present employees for the lessons you have taught me along the way. You have all contributed to my experience as a leader, and I am forever grateful. Hopefully, I have contributed to your growth as well.

My mom was my first teacher of management and leadership. She taught me that as the leader, you are ultimately responsible for everything; that respect is earned; to take care of your employees and they will take care of you; and that great leaders take ownership of their employees' mistakes and celebrate their wins.

My coach and mentor of nearly twenty years, Bernie Stoltz, taught me early on in my career that organizations grow by growing their people. Allowing someone who is not happy or someone whose talents are not appreciated to stay does not serve anyone. It is best to support them to find a happy place elsewhere so they can be appreciated for their special talents.

In 2011, my partners, Jennifer Chevalier, Thomas Walsh, Kimberly Hubenette and I founded Virtual Training Innovation (VTI) on the simple mission to streamline training and inspire employees to be self-learners. VTI leverages technology to create a consistent recipe for success and improves the training process for not only the business owners but for everyone involved in the process. VTI is a state-of-the-art cloud-based training system, Our cloud-base portals make it effortless for all members of the team to stay up-to-date with the practice's policies, procedures and more importantly culture. By all team members being trained to their full potential, the organization can achieve the next level of efficiency and create a high performance culture.

This book is a continuation of VTI's mission. Both my co-author Jennifer Chevalier and I want support you so that every person you hire as a partner will grow, learn, inspire and transform into a leader leading leaders, in an organization filled with happy people who are passionate about creating your vision and maintaining your culture through shared core values. *Hire to Inspire* will support you in being a great leader, mentor and inspiration to those you will have the honor to lead. The book is filled with resources that can support you on your journey to a happy work environment of employees who see themselves as partners. Finally, thanks to expert copyeditor Linda Jay for polishing the text until it glows (lindajay@aol.com.)

> With gratitude,
> Yolanda Mangrum, DDS, MAGD
> COO of Virtual Training Innovations and
> CEO of Petaluma Dental Group

[1]*The State of the Global Workplace: A Worldwide Study of Employee Engagement and Wellbeing*, Gallup Consulting, ©2010 Gallup Consulting.

Hire to Inspire

Chapter 1

Positive "I Can" Self-Talk
A Conversation with Steven Campbell

"Whether you think you can, or can't, you're right."[1]
- Henry Ford

In this chapter, we focus on the work of Steven Campbell, M.S.I.S., author of *Making Your Mind Magnificent.*[2] Campbell explains the concept of "self-talk," the importance that positive self-talk is to being successful, and how destructive negative self-talk is. As you will learn, you can do and become whatever you believe you can; at the same time, you can't do whatever you believe you can't.

Your brain believes whatever you tell it. While you are speaking with someone, you are talking to yourself three times faster than you can speak and when you are alone, you talk to yourself six times faster. This "self-talk conversation" determines how we see ourselves and creates our self-image of how we see ourselves in the world. We have thousands of self-images in our brain. Self-talk also affects our feelings, and links meanings to our emotions. Our thoughts have a profound effect on our emotions, both positive and negative.

It's no coincidence that we start our book with a discussion on self-talk, self-image and self-confidence, and creating an "I can" attitude. Becoming a great leader requires overcoming the hurdle that self-talk can create, whether it's your own personal self-talk or the self-talk each member of your team has regarding a particular belief. Changing that self-talk and using it to effect positive change is vital to becoming a great leader; fortunately, we can choose to make that change.

The prefrontal cortex in our brain gives us the ability to think, and distinguishes us from other animals. We can utilize our thoughts to refine and guide our emotions. Recognizing that we have the power to change our thoughts and hence gain control over our feelings is a first step to a positive self-image. It's not easy, of course; we have been under the influence of our thoughts for so long that we're not always aware of the general tone of our

1

thinking, nor do we realize that we have a choice. Another important point to understand is that "we behave and act not according to the truth, but the truth as we believe it to be." This "truth" refers to the thousands of self-images we have stored in our subconscious. Campbell further contends that if the "truth" about ourselves is less than our actual potential, what we can do, or become, or grow into, we behave accordingly.

Your self-confidence is built on how you see yourself in the world, your self-image. How do you build that self-confidence? Quite simply, change how you are talking to yourself. The reference for how you see yourself is what you have told your brain. The exciting thing is that we can tell our brains that 1+1 equals anything; research has discovered that our brains accept what we tell ourselves without question. You have heard the concept of self-defeating thought. If you tell yourself, "I am not good at _____," then your brain does exactly what it needs to accept that truth and make it a reality. On the other hand, when you say, "I am good at _____ ", or, "I can do _____", your brain ventures to find ways to make this the truth without question. The only problem is, the brain does not like change or being outside our comfort zone. Campbell says, "It will resist any changes you want as much as it can, and will find all sorts of ways of doing so, including telling you things about yourself that are simply not true." However, while it is difficult, we can reprogram our brains to embrace change and motivate us. *Making your Mind Magnificent* is a guidebook to teach your mind to be a motivator, mentor and trusted advisor working for you and not against you.

Our conscious mind holds the perception of information and our subconscious stores the information we call the "truth," a different version for each of us. It's in our subconscious that we create who we think we are, and then behave accordingly. This is done without ever asking if what you think about yourself is true, which is why change can be so difficult. However, there is also virtually no limit to the amount your brain can learn.

The primary element of what holds us back is not how old or how smart we are, it is what we say to ourselves. You are continually learning. Everything that you are and everything that you can do is based on how you see yourself, on your self-image. Taking that a step further, everything that you are is what you are telling yourself today. This is exciting, because it means that tomorrow you can change what you decide to say to yourself and can become whatever you believe you can become. Campbell recommends the book *Good to Great* [3] by Jim Collins, which introduces the rubric "Good is the

Enemy of Great," and illustrates how we don't have great relationships because we settle for good relationships. This translates into Campbell's concepts: we don't have great self-images because we settle for good self-images.

Campbell emphasizes that most of us pass over our successes far too quickly for them to ever become a part of our self-image. We downplay our successes because we feel it would be too egotistical to acknowledge "I was just lucky," or, "It's not that big of a deal." To be great, you must acknowledge your victories, and to be a great leader, you must acknowledge others' victories, celebrating them, making them part of your and your team's self-image. If you tell yourself, "It was just luck, I'm not really that good," your brain will believe it. Your success then is not repeatable or sustainable, and can't become a part of who you are.

Worse, we naturally wallow in our negative attributes by saying things to ourselves like, "How could I be so stupid?" You start listing all the stupid things you've ever done to validate why you are so stupid. Campbell emphasizes that we need to "throw away the list..." because your brain will record it as a current event and not something that you learned and improved from. You set yourself up for a vicious cycle, a loop wherein you can't learn from the event. Instead, say to yourself, "The next time, I will do it this way." First, you are saying that there will be a next time; we can have as many next times as we want. Second, you are giving yourself permission to make a mistake, in other words, permission to learn. Do not give up. Absolutely, you can control your self-talk and therefore your self-image, and the only exception is when you say you can't.

Another important self-talk concept to realize is that, as Campbell puts it, "Worrying is negative goal-setting." The brain locks in on what we are saying to ourselves and looks for ways to make it happen so that we put energy toward creating what we are worrying about. To change this, you must remain in the present and focus positive thoughts on the outcomes you want. Obviously, there are always going to be bad things that come up in life, but the advice is not to create problems.

How can leaders support their employees to have more positive self-talk? Leadership is based not only on your ability to communicate the vision and mission your company has to your employees but also your positive self-talk about the company. Employees follow the leader's self-talk. Leaders must master their self-talk, especially when things go wrong, because this is when employees are looking for the most support. In *Making Your Mind Magnificent*

Hire to Inspire

[2] Campbell discusses the work of psychologist Dr. Martin Seligman, who researched learned optimism for more than 20 years. Generally speaking, there are two habits of thinking, pessimism or optimism, which are defined by how people react when things happen in their lives.

	Good Event	Bad Event
Pessimism	1. Temporalize it 2. Isolate it 3. Believe they don't deserve the credit	1. Eternalize it 2. Globalize it 3. Believe it is all their fault
Optimism	1. Eternalize it 2. Globalize it 3. Believe they did it all	1. Temporalize it 2. Isolate it 3. Believe it is not all their fault

Campbell states that although pessimists can learn to be more optimists, "this transformation does not take place through simply whistling a happy tune, or mindless platitudes.... Your mind won't be fooled by that." The key takeaway is that employees are looking for leaders to be a positive example, especially when things are not going well.

To move your team through a negative or problem-solving process, Campbell recommends three steps:

1. **Isolate the problem** (Acknowledging it is not global. This one part is not going right; that doesn't mean the whole company is falling apart.)
2. **Temporalize the problem** (We will get out of this. We will find an answer. This will not last forever.)
3. *No blame* (What do we need to do so this won't happen again? Make sure no one is blaming or judging others or themselves.)

We recommend that leaders utilize these three brilliant steps to pre-frame any "problem" or opportunity that demands attention before addressing it with your employees. Adding this conversation allows for a more positive problem-solving response rather than an emotional, blaming or defensive response.

In conclusion, remember this quote from Steven Campbell: "The primary element that prevents or holds us back is our beliefs." Our brain has a captive audience, and we are the only one who gets to listen to it. What you are telling yourself does not become a part of you until you agree with it. The brain is like a computer program and runs programs that tell it $1+1=$ whatever.

Campbell's research tells us we can upload new programs, delete old ones that no longer serve us and, if necessary, change our whole operating system to adapt and grow. Does this mean that we can change people or employees? No! Only they have the power to accept change and load or delete programs in their brain. As the saying goes, "You can lead a horse to water but you can't make it drink." This is why hiring for the "I can" attitude is so key. Leaders don't change employees' self-talk, but we can show them a different path, an easier way to perform a particular task. We cannot change their self-image or self-confidence.

Leaders can teach employees how to think optimistically. Most people don't realize that can change the message they are telling themselves. Leaders can reinforce a positive environment for growth and change for team culture that builds self-confidence through acknowledgment. The key concept is to realize that motivation is an internal state, much like emotions and attitudes that only the individual can control. This leaves us with the sage advice: hire for attitude and train for skill.

When hiring, we recommend that leaders identify the candidate's passion, optimism, and what motivates them. Hire happy people with healthy self-images and the self-confidence to achieve winning results for your organization.

Great interview questions that will give you the insight to know if candidates are a good fit:

1. What are the most important decisions you have made in your life or career?
2. What are your life vision and goals?

VTI's self-learning platform supports the "I CAN" attitude by allowing team members to learn on their own time, and at a pace that is right for them. With over 100 hours of continuing education, and over 250 templates for business documents, YOU CAN run your practice with greater ease.

BIOGRAPHY

Steven Campbell is an author, speaker and mentor. As an award-winning author of the book, *Making Your Mind Magnificent,* Campbell teaches audiences how to flip negative thinking, embrace change, and realize their dreams simply by understanding how our brains function.

After working in hospital administration for twenty years, Steven Campbell acquired his Masters at the University of San Francisco and went on to pursue his greatest love, teaching. As both a university professor and educational dean in northern California for another 20 years, he now presents easy to understand principles about the brain that can be immediately applied to improve the quality of our thoughts and lives. Steven writes columns in *The Community Voice, The Christian Bee and Napa Valley Life Magazine* and is author of *Making Your Mind Magnificent – Flourishing at Any Age.*

Chapter 2

Being The Role Model -
The Leadership Characteristics Of Excellence
A Conversation with Lois Banta, Rhonda Savage
and Linda Miles

*"A good leader takes a little more than his share of the blame,
a little less than his share of the credit."*
- Arnold H. Glasow

In this chapter, we touch on the necessary leadership characteristics it takes to create a team-driven, participatory-owned organization. Team-driven means the people involved are motivated, enthusiastic and know the direction they are headed. Participatory ownership is when people who are affected by a decision are invited to share in the decision-making process and are committed to owning their actions. In organizations that have participatory ownership, leaders lead leaders. Imagine what it would be like in your organization to have leaders leading leaders at every level! This is the purpose of *Hire to Inspire*, and as you read through each chapter, you will learn how to become the role model for leaders leading leaders.

We interviewed three exceptional leaders who exemplify leadership and are role models, walking their talk. Lois Banta is the CEO of Banta Consulting, with over 30 years of experience coaching leaders to "See, commit and implement, moving them from mediocrity to excellence." Rhonda Savage is the CEO of Miles Global, and specializes in growing leaders and building stronger and happier teams. Linda Miles, Founder of Linda Miles & Associates and Founder of the Speaking Consulting Network, has been mentoring leaders since 1978 and believes "To rest is to rust." She has the experience and passion to lead leaders to excellence. These exceptional leaders will tell you the must- have leadership characteristics it takes to excel, and to consistently have winning results. It is so important to have a strong leader, for the growth of both your people and your organization. Lois, Rhonda and Linda also advise us on what to look for when adding a team member.

Hire to Inspire

What does it take to be a great leader? Leadership is one of those nebulous terms that has as many different meanings as there are personalities. We will drill deep into what being a great leader and role model is, and why that is necessary for having a successful outcome. Linda Miles defines it, "Leaders must do five things to get team accountability: hire well, train well, trust and praise team members, and follow up." We will focus on each of these areas throughout *Hire to Inspire.*

The character traits that make up a great leader can vary, depending on the organization, team, manager and work environment. Each leader has his or her own innate individual style, and, in order to inspire others to follow, must learn to make their leadership style flexible to accommodate various individuals. The better leaders can know themselves and can read their people, the better they can lead them. Personalities, behaviors and attitudes will affect people differently and will demand different approaches to reach the desired outcome.

It is up to the leader to create a work environment that will inspire and motivate employees. Leaders who have a clearly defined vision of their goal and core values that govern their everyday actions will inspire employees to follow them. Great leaders don't micromanage; rather, they give employees space to grow and permission to make mistakes. After all, failures lead to learning and eventually to successful outcomes. Leaders motivate employees by holding them accountable and by giving them recognition for their contributions. A highly motivated team requires little supervision, is highly productive and creates a pleasant work environment.

When asked what the top leadership traits or qualities they felt a strong leader must have, Lois, Rhonda and Linda responded:

Hire to Inspire

Lois	Rhonda	Linda
Integrity	Integrity	Vision
Enthusiasm	Honesty/ Trustworthy	Goal-Oriented
Trust	Caring	Trust/Respect
Ethics	Hard Work	Honesty/Integrity
Ability to Offer Hope Knowledgeable	Fair Good Listener	Patience Compassionate
Focus on team building	Excellent communicator	Management Habits that Add Fun to Work
Positive	Learner	Effective Communication
Solution-Oriented	Lead by Example	Flexibility
Creative	Optimistic	Passion for Success
Relationships	Influential	Appreciative

Interestingly, some traits were on all of their lists: integrity, honesty, trust, and effective communication, but if we asked twenty or twenty thousand other leaders, none would be exactly alike, and each would define the traits differently. It's important to recognize that depending on the environment, outcome and people, the leaders will need to adapt their approach as many times as it takes to get the results that they want. Leaders have to continually self-evaluate and measure their effectiveness. This is probably one of the most challenging parts to being a leader: you will never stop needing to develop your skills. In fact, like most things in life, leadership is a journey not a destination. The more leadership experience you have, the more you realize you don't know.

Let's listen to these experienced leaders to hear why they picked the traits they did.

Hire to Inspire

Rhonda: "I put integrity first on my list. I think it's good for a leader to express what the word integrity means to them; to me, integrity means doing the right thing, even when no one is looking. My second trait would be honesty. Third, I feel it's important to have a caring leader who expresses an interest in their people, and works at winning their hearts and minds. A caring leader gets people to do more. Hard work is a really important trait for a leader. Fairness is a really important quality. Leaders also need to be good listeners and good communicators. We don't train to be communicators in professional school or in many industries. Good leaders also need to be continual learners focused on wisdom and skills. Leaders should lead by example. They must fight negativity on a daily basis and constantly be optimistic. Good leaders are influential. They work at organization, but that doesn't mean they're always organized. It's difficult to get team members to work hard If the leader's office looks like a bomb's gone off in it; that sends the wrong message."

Lois: "I also listed number one as integrity. I think if you don't have integrity, it's difficult to be a really good leader. Enthusiasm is top on my list, because good leaders have to be enthusiastic and passionate about their purpose. They must gain trust and be trustworthy, and have good ethics for others to follow. They must have the ability to offer hope or solutions. They need to be knowledgeable about their skills. Leaders need to have a focus on building a good team unit and be positive and solution-oriented, with the ability to build nurturing relationships."

Linda: "I picked up some good traits from both Lois and Rhonda that I didn't have on my list. I can't believe I left off enthusiasm because that's the one thing we speakers hear the most. What do you do when the team's excited and the leader refuses to be enthusiastic? Number one on my list is leaders must have vision. If a leader doesn't know where he or she wants to be in five to ten years, how can that leader help the team get there? Visions, goals, trust and respect I put together. Honesty and integrity I also had on the same line. A good leader has to have patience. A lot of leaders become very frustrated. When people are learning, especially new employees, they definitely have to feel that the leader is going to be patient. Next on my list is compassion and appreciation for employees and for customers. Good time management habits are essential. I agree with Rhonda's example of organizational skills. If the leader's office looks like a bomb went off in it, the team members must assume that's okay for workplaces. Effective communication is really, really important. Having flexibility as a leader is important. Flexibility means if things aren't working and we've tried one system, or one way of doing things, then it's okay to back up and say this isn't working, let's regroup. Leaders have to show passion for success, because sometimes the team members tell us, 'I don't think our boss cares. I think he is burned out and happy with the status quo.' If team members see that the leader is not passionate about growing the business, they're not going be passionate, either."

All of these traits, and more, are essential to being a good or a great leader. To be a participatory leader (a leader who leads leaders), one must guide people and be inclusive. This style of leader will encourage and even empower employee input, team concepts and shared decision-making. The leader must listen to others, consider their ideas, and be humble enough to accept others' suggestions, as they may have a better alternative. It is important to remember, however, that the leader remains in charge and is the final decision maker. As the leader, you are not expected to know all the answers all the time; however, you are expected to make the right decisions with the information you have. So doesn't it make sense to gather honest feedback from those who may have solutions to a problem?

Strong leaders see themselves not as enforcers but rather as coaches, empowering the growth of their people in a caring and considerate way. Rhonda said, "To grow people, we've got to grow our leadership skills, and that takes time and energy." Can you agree with that? Leaders and team members must continually improve themselves. Lois added, "Strong leaders create great leaders within the team. Celebrating the successes of your team is crucial to building growth in an organization. Addressing challenges early allows the leader to not let them get out of control. Strong leaders have the ability to create a sense of 'ownership' in the team, therefore creating an environment for positive growth. Conflict is not a dirty word. You don't have to lead with an iron fist to address conflict."

Self-evaluation is a critical step for leaders. We must check in with ourselves regularly and with our team for feedback. There is always some area of leadership to work on. Recognizing and accepting that we as leaders are not perfect, and that we must continue to strengthen our skills, is an essential trait to role-model. Rhonda says, "A lot of times ego gets in the way of our ability to move forward, because we don't look at ourselves in depth and ask ourselves that huge leadership question, How am I doing? It is a self-accountability question and also a good one to ask your team." Rhonda suggests we be honest with our team about what particular area we as leaders struggle with and give them permission to coach us to be better. "We all struggle with leadership. We always have things to be working on. Let your team know, I'm going to ask you the question how am I doing, and I really appreciate honest feedback." That increases the leader's accountability to improving in that area. The leader's perception of themselves may be totally different from others' and so improvement may not happen. It's important to thank the team for their feedback; let them know you commit to working harder at improving this area and do not make excuses for your behavior. This is also role modeling at its best; it will show you are human and will build rapport and respect from your team.

Rhonda observes, "As a great leader, I'm willing to also say I'm sorry if I've made a mistake. People respect that. Ego can get in the way of being a great leader if he's not willing to listen to feedback." Of course, you have to be careful what the specific weakness area you choose to share is. The team needs to believe that you have the business under control so they can respect you enough to follow you. You might say that you are working on giving more positive feedback or on being a better communicator. Lois adds, "A leader shouldn't brag about cheating on their taxes if they want their team members to be honest. Walking their talk means displaying the traits they want their team to have."

Linda shared a personal story of her former boss, who was a "born leader." He told his team, "if you ever hear me say or see me do anything that you feel is offensive to a customer, one of your coworkers or you, it's your duty to write it down on a note and put it on my desk." What this told her and her colleagues was that he was willing to admit that he was capable of making mistakes and didn't have all the answers. She also shared that he came from "we" versus "you" when addressing areas that needed to be improved, which meant he was willing to say, I also need to improve and I need your help. Linda said, "Those are the four most powerful words that a leader can say to an employee. 'I need your help' means I don't have all the answers. That builds teams, accountability and empowerment. The leader may be in charge, but we are all part of the answer to the problem."

Employees want to fulfill their leaders' expectations and perform according to their standards. Positive feedback reassures and motivates them to be high performers. Generally, most employees would say they receive far more negative or corrective feedback than positive praise. Negative feedback can be demoralizing and demotivating if not coupled with praise. Praise costs you nothing and never really loses its effectiveness if it is genuine and sincere. Lois added, "One of my favorites is consistently checking in with each person and what you expect as results. I always say, inspect what they expect; if you want a good result, then you're going to have to walk that talk."

Rhonda shared a great story about an incredible mentor. "Years ago, I read an article about a schoolteacher in a very poor middle-school district where the kids had a high school graduation rate of 20-30 percent. The teacher thought, I can't change my school district or the poverty in the area. What I can change is my classroom, so to each kid she said, you have an A, and my job is to help you keep that A. If you bring me work that's not yet an A, we'll sit down and make sure that you know what needs to be done in order to get and keep your A. Her kids had a 70-80 percent high school graduation rate." Rhonda continued, "My goal for all our employees is to give them their A. We're clear up front about expectations. We provide training, prioritize work and set clear due dates so we know that we're accomplishing the prioritized work. A system of accountability is the job of a really good leader. People know where they stand and what they need to do, and that makes a huge difference."

Linda recommends a book by Cy Wakeman, "*Reality Based Leadership*,[7]" to every leader. The author says that empowerment without accountability is chaos. Linda says, "I firmly believe that it would be great if you could just give people assignments and know that they're going to be accountable." Leaders say to Linda, "Staff came to the seminar, or after the consultant came they were all fired up, but three or four weeks later, they were back to their old habits. How do you keep them accountable?" Hire well, train well, trust and praise them, and follow up.

She continues, "The missing link to most businesses is with office managers or the owner." If you hire me to reduce your accounts receivable by x number of dollars in 90 days, I can be very excited about my project. But if middle or upper management doesn't ask me how it's going, I'm only going to be accountable for a month. Outline your expectations, then take ten minutes a month to ask, how many calls did you make? What are the responses you're getting? What was your greatest aha on the collections? If they were not excited about my end results, I would lose enthusiasm."

Lois, Rhonda and Linda shared some great hiring advice for leaders on what to look for when adding to their team. Rhonda opened with, "I want a fire in their belly, I want somebody who's willing to learn and grow, and stretch. We know that about half of the applicants can be resistant to change. Yet right from the beginning, change is an expectation. We begin by asking them to step outside their comfort zone. We could ask during the application process, for them to write a 300-word essay on what excellent customer service is and what they want from a customer service experience standpoint. If they don't follow through, it shows lack of attention to detail. You can watch body language and behavior throughout the whole interview process. In my office, we use that customer service essay as one of those tools to see if somebody pays attention to details and if they really want the job. You know we're hiring first for attitude. You can't give somebody a good attitude or personality."

Lois continued, "You can train skills, but you can't train somebody to have a good attitude. I also write our ad to attract the right person for the job. Do not just put the job title, because you're going to get people who aren't necessarily the best fit for that position. So if you want to hire a rock star, then write the ad that way. I have seen managers make the mistake of hiring too quickly just because they get in this urgency trap and don't take personality into consideration. If you want to hire for a specific position in the office, then prepare a job description with specific job duties, so that when you interview the candidate you can have an intelligent conversation as to whether or not they qualify."

Linda adds, "It's important to "hire for attitude, personality, and appearance. Appearance does not mean movie star gorgeous or handsome: it means neatness. I'm a firm believer that people will do their work exactly the way they care for themselves. Being neat means they're going to take great pride in their customers, their work and their duties. There are three types of employees: those who are wiling and not able, which means they don't have the skill to do the job; those who are able but not willing, can do the job but do just enough to just get by; and those who are both willing and able to do the job, which is what you really are looking for, They are excited about the future of the business and making it grow. This narrows down further to givers or takers. A giver comes to work every morning with one thought -- what can I do for our customers, our organization and my coworkers to make this day easier, more productive and less stressful? A taker comes to work with the attitude: here I am, I'm absolutely dynamite, I can do it all, what time do I go to lunch? When's my next raise? And is it Friday yet? And as Lois said, you could attract the wrong employee with your ad; takers are attracted to a wonderful salary, corporate benefits, time off with pay, continuing education opportunities, and trips to Hawaii. So my ad would be, 'Would you like to be part of a team that truly cares about its customers and employees? If so, please apply for this job.' I think that most people are born caregivers and don't like money-driven organizations. Money comes if you do the right thing."

During the interview, Linda says, "To determine if the candidate is a giver or a taker, ask, if you received a gift of $200,000, what would you do with it? And if everything is about me, me, me, they're a taker, but if they think about it and say, 'I'd help my mom and dad pay off their mortgage, I'd send my parents on a trip; they've been so good to us children. I would set aside money for my children's education. I would pay off our bills. I would buy my husband the car he thinks can't afford,' hire them."

Finding team members that match your company's core values during an interview, Rhonda suggests that we first get really clear about what our company and personal values are. She recommends the leader have a values-driven exercise with their teams to get clear about the company values. Then during the interview, the leader asks the candidate what their core values are, then tells the candidate his or her own personal core values. Rhonda says an example is, "Integrity, which means doing the right thing even when no one's looking,"

Rhonda suggests a team interview process. "I love the team being involved in the interview process because how the candidate treats existing employees can be totally different than how they are with the leader, and, that's where you will see values. Remember, a real value isn't a value unless it exists even in hard times, and interviewing is a stressful thing for most people." Team interviews allow multiple perspectives to be observed.

Another question to ask a candidate: create a particularly difficult scenario in the work environment and ask, can you think of a time where you have resolved a similar situation? What happened? Looking back, how would you handle it now?" Generally speaking, leaders can tend to talk more than listen during interviews and ask close-ended questions. Leaders need to be active listeners during interviews, watch body language for sincerity, and ask a lot of open-ended questions.

Lois shared more advice on hiring. Prior to the interview, she suggests we create a list of interview questions specifically designed to identify good listening skills and a positive attitude. For example, Lois suggests, "Tell me about a time when you felt undervalued and unappreciated, when you didn't feel appreciated." It doesn't have to be with their last employer. I want them to be able to know how they express themselves, and if that is frustrating for them." Are they going to play a blame game? Do they own their part in the situation? What core values come from discussing this situation?

Linda added a couple of questions that she asks when interviewing to determine core values: "What was the most significant change or accomplishment you made in your last position?" and "What did you like most and like least about your former supervisor or leader?" I always tell my clients to beware of the person who bad-mouths their last office or their last leader, because you will be next to be bad-mouthed if you hire them. Beware if they come in with lots of baggage, because this is going to be a really short interview." Actively listening during the interview for how they communicate about others will give you the insight to know how likely they are to gossip, which, we would all agree, is "just so detrimental to any business."

For skill assessment, Rhonda suggests having a paid working interview. It does mean that you risk having them file for unemployment if you don't hire them, but there is no substitute to seeing them in action to test their skills; of course this would be as a final deciding step. "Within the hiring process we build in both the working interview and a 90-day training period. I prefer training period versus probation, which sounds like you're in jail. Included with this process, the leader performs 30-, 60-, and 90-day reviews. All employees need to know up front on a daily basis, specifically what they need to change and be appreciated for what they do well. But as soon as you know they are not the right fit, you should cut that person loose." Leaders say, I knew this person wasn't right three, four, five months ago, but yet wait for them to quit or for a better time to let them go. This is not good leadership, and it's not fair to you, to your team or to the employee to waste time in a place that does not have the need for, or appreciate, their talents. Time and time again we see people who are unhappy in their work but feel paralyzed about making a decision to leave. Leaders must have the courage to encourage unhappy people to leave their organization and then support them to find a happy situation. This is will be explored more in Chapter 5, when we discuss, from the employee's perspective, whom to hire, inspire or fire. Rhonda suggests that you read her article in *Dental Town* titled, "*I'm so sick of her attitude, I wish she'd just quit.*" Rhonda says leaders in general keep people too long, hoping that things will get better.

Lois adds, "I think you don't delay. If somebody's not working out, you shouldn't keep hoping for years it will change. I agree, hire slow, fire fast. I think you need to gift them with the opportunity to find another place to be happy. I've talked to many leaders after they've made the decision to let a team member go. The person came up to them and said wow, finally. If you choose to keep someone on who has negative behavior and is not doing their job, the rest of the team suffers because they are there for the right reasons. A drop of poison in a gallon of water makes a gallon of poison in a work environment." Lois encourages leaders to act the moment they know someone is the wrong person for the team so the "A-level" employees aren't poisoned. As soon as the decision is made and acted on, the environment changes and the team is more motivated to perform.

Linda added another great tip, "One of the things that I think many good leaders use with hiring is the DiSC behavioral profile as part of the final interviewing process. On the ideal team, people have different strengths and different weaknesses that complement one another. I went to a female doctor's practice 15 years ago; they were highly stressed and no fun. I was the SOS, save our ship, person. When we did the DiSC behavioral profile, the two female dentists were high C's, which is a perfectionist, off the chart. They create stress, and six out of the seven women on their team were high C's, so they didn't have a good blend of behavioral styles. I think DiSC is one of the most valuable tools out there. It lets you know if a person is going to have the strength that you're looking for in a particular position and if they're going to blend well with the coworkers."

One final point on leadership: Remember, it's important to always do the right thing at the right time and to let your people know why you are making a certain request. Let's close our discussion on leadership with some great quotes that motivate us and we hope will motivate you on your leadership journey.

Rhonda remarked, "I'm an intense, passionate kind of person and I don't want to overwhelm my people. That can drive morale down, so I say this to myself almost daily: 'Take your work seriously but yourself lightly,' by Bob Nelson. And another favorite is from Mark Twain: 'The difference between the almost right word and the right word is ... the difference between the lightning bug and the lightning.' It is how we choose our words that matter. We leaders need to be careful we send the right message in all our actions, and recognize that the words we use are part of that process."

Linda shared, "I always keep inspirational quotes in the back of my day planner. This is from Johann Wolfgang Von Goethe: 'If you treat an individual... as if he were what he ought to be and could be, he will become what he ought to be and could be.' This is powerful for a leader. My favorite leadership quotes from General Norman Schwarzkopf are, 'Leaders live in glass houses…your people watch you!' and 'You don't have to be liked as a leader, but you do have to be respected."

Lois is inspired by these two quotes, "If you think you can, or you think you can't, you're right," by Henry Ford. Another favorite is from Maya Angelou: "I've learned that people will forget what you said, people will forget what you did, but people will never forget how you made them feel." Lois says, "This quote is important for leaders to keep in mind, with their employees, and for employees, with their customers. Customer service is such an important part of business success."

The VTI portal allows each team member the ability to organize, store and develop their department tasks and systems by offering them a cloud-based filing cabinet and video library. Each team member is encouraged to store and create their business protocols for best practices, helping them to become leaders of their department.

BIOGRAPHIES

Lois Banta is CEO, President and Founder of Banta Consulting, Inc., a company that specializes in all aspects of dental practice management. Lois has over 37 years of dental experience; she consults and speaks nationally and internationally and is the owner and CEO of The Speaking Consulting Network. To inquire about Banta Consulting or The Speaking Consulting Network, contact: 816/847-2055, 33010 NE Pink Hill Rd., Grain Valley, Missouri 64029, Email: lois@bantaconsulting.com or check out her websites: www.bantaconsulting.com for more information on office consulting, training and retreats and www.speakingconsultingnetwork.com to find out about starting or enhancing their own speaking, consulting and writing careers.

Lois Banta's speaking presentations can help your practice thrive so that you can focus on the health and wellbeing of your patients. As a staff trainer, team builder and speaker, Lois effectively teaches the dental team how to move in the same direction while performing their individual tasks. Lois's presentations offer proven techniques to boost revenue, decrease stress, and build a positive atmosphere in which employees love their jobs and patients look forward to visits.

Hire to Inspire

Linda Miles, CSP, CMC, Virginia Beach, Virginia, is an internationally recognized consultant, speaker and author on dental practice and staff development. Linda founded LLM&A, a leading INC 500 dental management consulting firm, in 1978, and the Speaking Consulting Network in 1997. She sold those businesses in 2007 and 2010, to devote more time to the Oral Cancer Cause foundation (OCC) in 2013. Linda has spoken in all 50 states and on four continents, authored three books and mentored many dental consultants. Go to: www.AskLindaMiles.com. or www.oralcancercause.org. Linda can be reached at lindamiles@cox.net or at 757-721-3125.

After retiring from in-office consulting and all-day lectures in 2013, Linda Miles co-founded (with her business partner, Robin Morrison of Florida), a nonprofit foundation to financially assist oral cancer patients after diagnoses and during their medical treatments. This debilitating disease, which took the lives of Linda's sister-in-law Charlotte and Robin's brother Mike in the same year (2012) is their legacy. Oral cancer kills one person each hour. By OCC creating an awareness of the importance of early diagnosis and involving the dental community in sharing the workload of this important endeavor, OCC will save lives and make a huge difference for future generations. Visit the OCC site and make a small donation in honor or memory of a friend or loved one.

Dr. Rhonda Savage is the CEO of Miles Global, an international dental training and consulting firm. Her speaking and publishing topics include women's health issues, leadership and business management.

Her 35 years in dentistry include roles as a dental assistant, a front office staff member and a private practice dentist. Dr. Savage understands the demands of quality patient care, leading a winning team and running a successful business.

Dr. Savage brings a unique energy to her work. A Lieutenant Commander in the Navy during the years of Desert Shield and Desert Storm, she received the Navy Achievement Medal and an Expert Pistol Medal, earning her the nickname of "The Beast." She's a "straight shooter," aiming her knowledge at the critical issues that dental practices face today. Visit www.MilesGlobal.net for her training products. If you'd like her to speak to your organization or provide consulting services, call 877-343-0909.

Hire to Inspire

Chapter 3

Telling the Story of Why and Having a Clear Vision
A Conversation with Fred Joyal

"All our dreams can come true, if we have the courage to pursue them.
- Walt Disney

Working on a team with clear vision, a common goal and a common purpose is one of the most rewarding experiences an employer or employee can have. Successful leaders can make any dream or vision come true when they can hire and inspire people to align and find their own purpose in making their vision a reality. As motivational speaker Zig Ziglar says, "True joy comes when you inspire, encourage, and guide someone else on a path that benefits him or her." There's no limit to what great teams will accomplish when aligned with a common purpose and a trusted leader to guide them. On the other hand, working without a clear direction or common purpose will leave you and your team lost, dissatisfied and frustrated.

In this chapter, Fred Joyal, the Founder of 1-800-Dentist® and Chairman of Futuredontics Incorporated, will encourage leaders to communicate the *why* behind their vision so that the team can move in the same direction to meet the company's objectives. He shares his first-hand experience of being an entrepreneur and understands the importance of communicating your vision to your employees. Joyal says it's not sufficient to just have a vision statement; you have to explain the *why* to engage the entrepreneurial spirit of your employees. If employees don't understand the *why*, they cannot utilize their talents to get the job done. Fred will also support leaders in defining their vision and add his insight and wisdom about hiring.

Why It's Important to Have a Clear Vision

"If you don't know where you're going, any road will get you there."
- Lewis Carroll, author, Through the Looking Glass

Gallup's 2010[4] report found that only thirty percent of the U.S workforce is engaged in their work and love what they do. Seventy percent are "not engaged" or "actively disengaged," meaning they hate their jobs or are, at best, unenthusiastic about their roles. From the same Gallup report: "When organizations successfully engage their customers and their employees, they experience a 240 percent boost in performance-related business outcomes, compared with an organization with neither engaged employees nor engaged customers."

As Joyal says, leaders have to know where they're going to get anywhere in business. Without a clear vision, it's very easy for people to just show up and "do" their job, perhaps even stay busy and think that's enough to earn their paycheck. The problem is, that's not rewarding; exchanging their time for dollars doesn't keep employees engaged. It's hard for employees to remain inspired when they have no specific goals or objectives for strategic priorities. After all, if you don't have a clear destination, how will you and your employees get there?

It's up to the leader to say, "We're going here and this is why." In the end, though, it takes a team to realize the business vision. All team members need to know the "where, what and why" based on the clear vision articulated by the leader. Joyal: "It's not enough to just have the vision, however. It has to be understood by everyone and explain the purpose of the business." Many businesses have a vision statement posted for employees and even customers to read, but it isn't well understood. In fact, you could ask employees, "What are we doing here, why are we here, what's the purpose of this business?" One hundred employees will give 100 different answers.

In contrast, successful businesses have a clearly articulated vision that everybody knows. The vision statement is memorable. The vision purpose guides them through their work day, including their interaction with customers. Joyal points out, "The most important part of a vision is, employees have to know why and what the business stands for." Otherwise, employees will not be able to wholeheartedly support business policies or procedures. They may even give customers the wrong impression of the business.

Hire to Inspire

Responsibility lies with the leader to articulate the vision; it is up to the employees to execute on that vision. Employees will have a sense of the purpose of the business and defined roles; no more hiding in cubicles. They are part of the organism and they understand what the entire organism's function is. Job satisfaction, motivation and engagement support the success of the business because employees are proud of their work and contribution. This is initiative, innovation and ownership when employees start asking, "What can I do to make this business better today?" Being a contributor and making a difference is a much more satisfying life as an employee.

Joyal says that generally, business leaders are creating jobs for people who don't want to own their own business. Most people don't want to have to figure it out or take all the risks or make all the decisions, but they do want to participate and help execute the vision, once they realize what it is. Employees' satisfaction comes from being team players, having a greater purpose. Studies have shown that the Number One thing that sparks better performance is greater clarity about what the organization needs and wants employees to do, and why. Employee engagement is both the rational and the emotional connection of an employee with the organization's vision/core purpose that jibes with their willingness to give extra effort. Engaged employees who are enabled to create exceptional service experiences will give businesses a real and sustainable competitive advantage.

Creating a Vision

Any good business succeeds because it solves a unique problem for customers, whether it's a great vacation or great customer service or a great set of tires for their car. It always comes down to understanding what business you're in and what problem you're solving. Joyal's business solves the difficult problem of finding a dentist you're going to love. He based the need for 1-800-Dentist® on having a really terrific dentist in the 1980s and wondering, "How would anybody would find this guy? I was lucky. I stumbled upon him. I came in to solve the problem."

Of course once you have written your business priorities down, then you must verbalize them. Joyal emphasizes, "I say this over and over again to my own team, and to anybody else who's starting a business. If the purpose of your business is to make money, just stop now, because you have such a poorly defined sense of what your business is actually for, or your priorities are so imbalanced, that you are unlikely to succeed in the long term."

Your business has to be able to solve somebody's problem. When you are leading employees in a business, this has to be defined through the vision/core purpose. The vision must tell employees the value the business creates for the customer, why this is important and how it will be accomplished.

The first step is to answer these questions: What is our business's daily purpose? What problem are we going to solve? Then put that into a concise, easy-to-remember, well-articulated format. Oftentimes it is a good idea to collaborate with your team to wordsmith the vision; as co-creators, they will take more pride and ownership. Articulate the results you hope your office will achieve in a way that inspires your employees. The vision will act as a guideline everyone can follow, on how to make the right decisions in day-to-day operations. Incorporating your vision into practice means you have your vision statement posted, visible for both employees and customers to see, regularly review the statement in team meetings and evaluate yourselves on meeting your vision. The vision is first introduced at the interview and emphasized throughout training as the beacon that joins everyone together. Employees' job descriptions should have individual strategic objectives that will contribute to your business's overall vision. The vision becomes part of the essential lexicon of the business, and it's part of the conversation as you're developing a product or adding a feature. Everybody should be trained to turn to it as a reference point and utilize it as a measurement tool to tell them whether they're on-track or off-track.

Visions evolve as the business grows, so you have to continually evaluate the vision for accuracy. Joyal says to consider your vision as your own "little lighthouse" for keeping your direction straight and on-course. When making goals and setting up procedures, monitor how they stand up against your business vision and utilize them as a litmus test to see if they take you closer to realizing your vision without compromising your integrity or core values. Visions need to incorporate core values, "what you will and won't do for money." Core values articulate various aspects of corporate behavior and further elucidate what you're there for, and what you will and won't do for money, specifying what trumps what. A great example of business vision and core values is from Zappos, the online shoe company. Founder Tony Hsieh created Zappos with a clear vision and strong core values. We recommend you read his book *Delivering Happiness* [8] to grasp the full culture of his company, exemplifying how day-to-day behavior is guided by vision and core values.

We will go into a deeper conversation of core values in our next chapter.

Leader's Role in Implementing Vision

A leader:

- clearly communicates the *why* behind decisions and frequently reiterates the vision, not assuming that everybody knows it;
- maintains core values and keeps a clear vision by having the courage to always do the right thing at the right time;
- is predictably consistent, so anybody following him or her knows exactly how the leader will respond by not giving mixed signals or contradictory messages;
- knows failures are learning opportunities and doesn't expect his team to be perfect;
- sees failures as information. Joyal says, "With success, you could've gotten lucky. Failure's full of information." Henry Ford drives this point home further when he said: "Failure is simply the opportunity to begin again more intelligently."
- celebrates the people around them and gives the team all the credit for success while taking all the blame for failure; General Eisenhower's leader exemplified this in the chilling letter he drafted in case the Nazis won on D-Day where he was quoted to say, "Our landings in the Cherbourg-Havre area have failed to gain a satisfactory foothold and I have withdrawn the troops. My decision to attack at this time and place was based upon the best information available. The troops, the air and the Navy did all that bravery and devotion to duty could do. If any blame or fault attaches to the attempt, it is mine alone." [9]
- continually self-evaluates whether they're walking their talk;
- creates a safe place for trusted advisers to tell them where they're messing up or where they're weak. (A book that will support leaders with self-evaluation and leadership is *What Got You Here Won't Get You There* by Marshall Goldsmith. [10])
- hires to counterbalance their own weaknesses and for the skills they need to fulfill their vision. Creates the path to growth by adding value and developing their employees. When leaders value their employees as talent and encourage them to contribute, innovation

and creativity occurs;

- creates a safe place to work where customers won't treat their people disrespectfully. Recognizes "the customer isn't always right" and that sometimes it's necessary to "fire" customers to protect your employees from being mistreated;
- is consistent and systematic in performance appraisals, regularly giving both praise and corrective feedback where it's due;
- demands more from the employees than they think they're capable of giving, by believing in them so they will strive beyond their perceived limitations and continue to better themselves;
- gets his or her "hands dirty" by interacting and being a part of operations, and never puts more than three layers of employees between him or her and the customer;
- protects his culture and supports his team by hiring slow and firing fast. Gets to know the candidate and makes the hiring process a team process. The minute he knows it's not working out, is quick to self-correct and support the culture and the team by firing fast. Many times the team will thank you and sometimes the person you are firing will thank you, too, because they know they are not a good fit and deserve to be where they will be appreciated.

Hiring Advice from Fred Joyal

"Begin with the end in mind." Joyal's first speech to welcome new hires is, "I hope you stay here a long time, but when you leave, you will be a better employee for any company than you are right now because you're going to have more skills; you're going to know how to work better in an organization; you're going to have challenged yourself the whole time you're here." Incorporating this speech into your onboarding process will set the stage and engage new hires at the level of interaction you will be expecting and will let them know you are making an investment in them. Most will feel appreciative and will be more likely to stay with you.

Before you can place the help wanted ad, you must first know your culture and the vision you are looking to create. Evaluate and implement the vision you have for your culture. Make sure everyone knows your vision including the applicant. What's the culture that you're trying to create? Is it fun? Hard-working? Creative? Incredibly supportive/ Incredibly competitive and challenging? When hiring people, you need to know the culture to know what you are looking for; and, you want to spell out the culture to the people you are looking for, in the ad, and again in the interview.

Lay out your expectations from the beginning. In order for candidates to be able to agree to perform the job at the level you want, they need to know the company vision, core values, culture and job expectations.

In your help wanted ad, be specific about the desired qualities of the candidate, business, environment and the job. Personality, skills, experience, values and characteristics all need to be defined. What is your company culture like? Paint a picture of the day-to-day needs and expectations of the job; the more specific you are, the more likely the applicant can honestly respond. Avoid generalizations like team player, great attitude and great communicator.

Get as much information during the application phase as possible by having candidates write short essays about their personal experiences and goals. This will enable you to know how they work and their level of motivation. Additionally, as part of the application process, administer a personality test, which will support you in matching job skills to the candidate.

Be very slow to hire. We all are so eager to plug that hole, but we need to be more judicious in finding just the right person to match the skill, culture and personality of the job. Leaders must see themselves as protecting the team and preserving the culture in the hiring process. Personality tests are important, as are multiple interviews with multiple interviewers, because they will each get a different perspective. Joyal, however, does not recommend having a "gang approach" to interviewing. He says to do the interviews individually, with each interviewer giving their own impressions of the candidate.

Be open to all possibilities; sometimes you find talent from within by re-sorting the team into different roles or locations; sometimes people who apply for one job are better suited for another job.

Hire people who are motivated, and then inspire them! It's not just hire for attitude, it's hire motivated people. As we've read in previous chapters of this book, people's natural inclination is to do only what it takes not to get fired. A great quote from inspirational speaker, Simon Sinek, "Great companies don't hire skilled people and motivate them; they hire already motivated people and inspire them. People are either motivated or they are not. However, unless you give motivated people something to believe in, something bigger than their job to work toward, they will motivate themselves to find a new job and you'll be stuck with whoever's left."

Interview questions:

- *Have you ever worked somewhere where you felt like you didn't fit? What was that like for you? What was the environment like?* Take this to a deeper level by asking more questions after hearing the answers to this and to the personality test.
- *Do you think of yourself as a highly punctual person?* This question tells the candidate that punctuality is important in your business.
- *Do you smoke?* You choose not to hire somebody who needs to go outside and smoke sometimes five or more times a day.
- *What was the worst mistake you ever made, and what did you learn from it?* This question will reveal an openness to learning from mistakes.
- *When you get out of bed in the morning, what do you say to yourself?* This will tell you if the person is optimistic, motivated or excited. Does he dread getting up? Does he hate the drive to work?

 Tell the story of your "Why" through a video. It's also a wonderful way to introduce new team members to your practice's Mission Statement and reintroduce your purpose to your existing staff. Uploading your videos in your VTI portal is easy and fun!

BIOGRAPHY

Alfred (Fred) Joseph Joyal is an entrepreneur who partnered with Gary Saint Denis in 1986 to form the successful dental referral service, 1-800-DENTIST. As the company's spokesman, he has written over 200 television and radio commercials and interacted with thousands of the most successful dentists across the country. Fred has lectured at national and local dental industry trade shows and has been published in a variety of prominent trade publications. Under Fred's leadership, 1-800-DENTIST has matched millions of consumers with the right dentist, giving him unique insight into the mindset of the modern dental patient. Today he serves as the chairman of Futuredontics, Inc., which operates 1-800-DENTIST as well as several other brands, and is regarded as one of the world's leading experts on dental consumer marketing. Fred can be contacted via email at fred@1800dentist.com. Follow his blog at www.GoAskFred.com.

Chapter 4

Core Values - Lead by Example:
Conversations with Joseph Stith and Bob Leonard

"If you hire people just because they can do a job, they'll work for your money. But if you hire people who believe what you believe, they'll work for you with blood and sweat and tears."
- Simon Sinek

As we have read previously, leaders with vision and values inspire employees. In this chapter we will discuss why it is important to have defined and articulated company core values. This gives employees a compass so they know how to contribute best to the company on a daily basis. We will also focus on hiring strategies for matching team members' personal core values with the company's core values. Our contributors in this chapter are so passionate about core values that they translate this to an even deeper meaning: core values are governing values and the honor code for living your life.

Joseph Stith has over 20 years of experience as an executive growth and development consultant. Robert Leonard is an executive coach at Fortune Practice Management and a former Marine officer. Both agree that leaders must continually improve their leadership skills and be willing to give their team permission to hold them accountable in maintaining their stated core values. It's imperative to select team members whose personal core values match the company's core values.

Core values mean different things to different people. Inspirational values that many people share in the workplace include:
- respect for each other;
- honesty and integrity -- the leader does what she says she's going to do, whether dealing with employees or customers;
- fairness without favoritism in dealing with your employees and being sure that they understand the basis for your decisions, the *why*.

Employees who are treated with respect, honesty, and fairness will return that loyalty to an organization, reflected in their dealings with others. People

31

will leave a company solely based on the clash of the company's core values with their personal values. Conversely, people will join an organization solely because they believe in its core values.

Joseph Stith prefers to call core values "governing values, values that govern all of us at the core," which is easier for people to understand. He says that he "loves history because it adds context to so much of what we do." Stith believes that the story of our Constitution is instructive for understanding the power of core values. "Once we had independence, the Articles of Confederation were no longer working. We were losing the country, and the great visionaries like Jefferson and Benjamin Franklin recognized that if we didn't get the governing values of this country right, we were in jeopardy of losing everything."

In 1726, at the age of 20, Benjamin Franklin created a system to develop his character and virtue. His goal was to arrive at perfection. "When Benjamin finished these twelve attributes, or values, he took them to a Quaker friend and explained his goal, saying, 'You know me better than anyone; what do you think?' His friend said, 'It's really good, but you're missing one, humility.' He went on to explain to Benjamin the specific places in which he was lacking in humility. Benjamin agreed, and added humility."

After that, Franklin committed to giving strict attention to one virtue each week; after thirteen weeks, he had moved through all thirteen. Then he would start the process over again and in a year, he had completed the course a total of four times. He tracked his progress by using a little book with thirteen charts. Every evening he would put a dot next to each virtue with a related fault he had committed that day. His goal was to live without any marks on his chart. Over time he improved, but he always carried the little book with him as a reminder.

Stith says, "By the time Franklin went to the Constitutional Convention, he was in his eighties. He had spent more than 50 years practicing and internalizing what it means to establish a set of core values, bringing his personal performance closer to those values on a weekly and daily basis. Franklin had a tremendous influence on why that was necessary for an entire nation, to put this into our governing doctrine, the American Constitution. Hence, the Constitution is a set of values, and we have been trying to compare our performance to those standards for hundreds of years now. When we say that something is unconstitutional, what we're really saying is, it is inconsistent with our values."

The key leadership takeaway is that core/governing values are important and require self-discipline, and self-evaluation of our daily actions. When leaders are consistent in following their beliefs, and walk their talk, people respect them and will follow them if they hold the same personal values.

Developing company core/governing values starts with the leader determining his or her personal values. If you are the owner and leader of the company, then your personal values are the company's values and should be stated as *"Company X's Core Values set by Leader X's Personal Core Values."* This says that you as the leader are willing to be held personally responsible for upholding these core values, with all your daily actions setting the company's policies and standard operating procedures.

For example:
   "Company X's Core Values set by Leader X's Personal Core Values."

Relationships
   • Based on trust, meaning no lies or leaving out pertinent information.
   • Must take ownership of own action.
   • Take immediate action on needs for correction.

Work
   • Family values are important, treat team as people, team support is a given, we work together to support each other.
   • Efficient and effective use of time.
   • Celebrate Wins!

Ethical/Morals
   • Never compromise on the safety of customers or team.
   • Never disrespect co-workers and always have their backs.
   • Never recommend services that I would not be comfortable giving to a loved one.

To create personal core values, we suggest that you ask yourself the question, "What do I value so much that wavering from it would be a deal-breaker for me and considered intolerable?" It is also a good idea to to get more specific about your values categories, like relationships, work and ethical/moral.

After you have your top three-to-five core/governing values in each category:

1. Present them to your team.
2. Tell them that you would consider wavering from these values intolerable.
3. Say that your intention is to always live up to these values.
4. Say that you recognize you're not going to be perfect.
5. Ask them to support you on reaching these standards by telling you if anything you do violates any of these values.
6. Ask them to take time to write down three-to-five personal core values in each category that they would consider intolerable.
7. As a team, have them review their personal core values; do any of them resonate as values that the company needs to add to its list?
8. File each team member's personal core values in a team binder as a resource, to help understand them better.
9. Publicly post the company's core values and regularly ask the team how are we doing and how can we improve?
10. Make a list of your growth opportunities and commit to focusing on them.

Stith says to keep in mind that, "Some people go through this very quickly, and others take a while to internalize this." It's important for each statement to be definitive and not "I will try to" or "I want to." However, he warns, "If you never share your company core values with anyone, it's powerful. But the real power comes when an organization develops the values they expect and publishes them for the team, and sometimes for the customers. This allows others to hold the company accountable. Because if you never show them, no one knows what you really want and the standards are never upheld."

Understanding each other's personal core values will also provide you with knowledge about how to communicate more effectively and how to support each other in contributing full-out. Knowing your individual personal values also gives you the opportunity to hold the team accountable to the standards they have set, versus the values the company has imposed.

As Stith points out, "Just like we have with the Constitution of the United States of America as a standard, there's a lot of magic in your company's core values. Because now you have perspective, and you can compare where you are with where you want to be." You also have the governing principles you, as leader, hold as your constitution before implementing policies or procedures.

Further, this defines the structure by which all current and future employees are compared, to see if their values are congruent with the company's.

Reviewing core values regularly builds stronger companies and more respected leaders. As Stith says, "It's very powerful for a leader to say, 'I know I am not perfect, but I have rated myself, as I compare my performance to high standards. Would you do the same? And can I give you permission to hold me accountable when I don't measure up to the person that I want to be?' This is humility, and shows your people you do have high standards, but that you make mistakes too.

We asked Bob Leonard about core values. He says they simply come down to asking the question, "What you do believe in, as an organization or as an individual?" He worked with J. Walter Thompson, the largest and oldest advertising agency in the world, and has dealt with many organizations' core values. "Also, I'm heavily influenced by my first job out of college as an officer in the United States Marine Corps. The thing that separates the Marines, in my opinion, from the other branches of service is not their unique mission, but their culture. Marines believe that no matter what the sacrifice, they'll get the job done. And they will never surrender, they will never retreat, they will never leave somebody with the enemy, and they will do whatever's necessary to win the battle, because of their core values." Leonard suggests that whatever your core values are, you should find a provocative and innovative way to remind people what they are.

Core values are "what we would not stop doing. even though it cost our business or ourselves money. We believe in them so much," according to Leonard. He suggests exploring Simon Sinek's book *Start with Why,*[11] which illustrates the point that people will work harder for core values than for a paycheck. "People don't buy what you do; they buy why you do it. And what you do simply proves what you believe." Employees who see their work as a job work for money, but those who work for a cause will work with blood, sweat and tears.

Think of organizations with strong core values: Apple, Hewlett-Packard, Disney, West Point. What images come to mind? Bob Leonard shares the stories of how exceptional core values penetrate the employee culture.

- Steve Jobs, former CEO at Apple Computer, would say that Apple's core value is that they believe passionate people can make a difference and change the world. This has nothing to do with consumer electronics and computers. In fact, Apple challenges the status quo and does things differently, with easy-to-use, well-designed computers. That's why Apple attracts customers and employees who believe in the company. The core value gives a cause for people to believe in. Apple customers will stand in line for two weeks to get the next iPhone when they could buy one off the shelf two weeks later.

- David Packard, when he was in high school, worked in a mine in Colorado where his employer treated people like dirt. After this experience, Packard pledged he would never be part of an organization that treated people so badly. It was his deeply passionate belief in a core value, treating people with dignity and respect, that made Hewlett-Packard so successful.

- Walt Disney's vision for Disneyland was to be the happiest place on Earth. Ever since Disneyland was created in 1955, they have referred to employees as "Cast Members" whose role is to create happiness. and to make the guests happy. The core values of safety, courtesy, showtime and efficiency set their standards. Disney cast members are clear about their core values and do whatever it takes to make sure every Disneyland guest feels it's the happiest place on earth.

- The West Point motto is: duty, honor, and country, for which graduates are willing to die. West Point, like most of the service academies, gives all their first-year students, a book called *A Message to Garcia*,[29] by Elbert Hubbard. During the Spanish-American War, the President of the United States needs to get a message to a man named Garcia in Cuba. Supposedly Lieutenant Rowan, who works at the White House, is the best person to do that job. The president calls the lieutenant into the Oval Office but before he can explain what the message is, Rowan disappears and three weeks later delivers that message to Garcia.

If you're attending West Point or Annapolis, nobody's going to spoonfeed you and hold your hand. You're going to have to take the initiative and do the right thing. And if you can't, chances are you're not going to last very long there. The service academies also don't tolerate lying, cheating or stealing.

There is always more to learn as a leader. Consider these additional resources:

- *Good to Great*, by Jim Collins[3]

- *Five Dysfunctions of a Team*[12], by Patrick Lencioni
- *Start with Why*[11] by Simon Sinek, and also watch his TED talk
- Watch the movie *"Perfect Effort"*[13]

"Perfect Effort" is an award-winning documentary about Coach Bob Ladouceur and De La Salle High School in California football's 12-year, 151-game wins. This was the greatest winning streak in the history of American sports. The team culture is formed by their core values. Leonard refers to Coach Bob Ladouceur as "one of my other heroes."

The coach says he believes the culture that he has formed has nothing to do with winning a football game. It's all about perfect effort. What he means by that is, if you're a football player and you say you're going to block the guy in front of you, you do that, no matter what. "All I ask these kids to do is make their perfect effort. I never told them they have to win a game, just to make their individual perfect effort." For him, it's more than being on a winning football team, it's about how to be successful in life. Coach Ladouceur is a modest guy who believes in teaching young men how to live up to their commitments, and that every team has a collective character or heart, which is based on love. Put simply, in this case love means, you can count on me and I have your back.

A final comment on core values; if, as a leader, you are not really walking the talk based on your core values, then how is your team going to follow you? For a leader to be held accountable, he needs to have the courage to encourage his team to give him feedback. Leaders don't grow organizations, they grow people, and you're not going to do that if you're not living up to your core values.

About hiring, as Stith says, "When people talk, they always reveal their values, if you listen." Leaders attract employees who believe in their company core values, especially if they are articulated and visible.

When hiring, it's a good idea to see who on the team is the best at reading people's personalities, has the skill set to be a critical thinker, watches body language and observes closely for what is not being said. We would suggest that this person prescreen resumes and make first contact on the phone for initial interviews. If the candidate impresses them, the leader can conduct the next interview, with this person in the room as an observer. This process can narrow the pool down to two or three candidates who are the most competitive, to make the right decision to hire.

Final candidates should go to lunch with the team individually to see if they're the right fit. This helps leaders develop a participatory ownership culture, this team hiring process. The team is invested in the new hire and will invest in a solution if a problem arises, because they will feel responsible for making it work. If the new hire is not a keeper, the team supports the leader in being quicker to fire that person. This is an important process in helping a team develop by finding the right people with the right values.

Team members who are clear on the governing values of their organization are ambassadors and protectors of those values. And that's easier for the team to do than the leader, since he or she is relatively removed. However, they need to be involved, they need to empower the team to feel a sense of responsibility, obligation and trust. The greatest asset is your team.

Understand that marketing is as much about changing and growing as a organization and getting clear on who you are and the type of customer/client you want to attract, as it is about the strategies you use to market yourself.

We think of marketing as a strategy for convincing people to become your customer/client. But really it's showing people your value through your actions, and seeing your governing values. It's empowering to work for a leader you know trusts you enough to actually ask for your opinion. If the only time that happens is in a staff meeting, you as a leader may not find out the information you need to make changes. You're not trying to turn your staff into whistle-blowers, but if there's a problem, they will tell you if you've created an environment of trust.

Let's say the organization creates the core/governing values for their organization. Too often we go through the process, write it down, stick it in a drawer and never look at it again. We write the mission statement down and hang it on the wall. But the customers don't read it, and we don't read it. We don't even know if we even believe in it anymore.

In a team meeting, there might be one core value that we focus on every month, and read in each meeting. Maybe you would assign a team member to speak on the core value, on a rotating basis, about where you think we measure up. Where have we failed and where have we succeeded?

So the topic of core/ governing values is always on the table in an office, like Benjamin Franklin did when he made his governing values and rotated them on a weekly basis. Then it becomes part of our culture, except we don't know how to build culture. What I just described is how you build the culture you need in an organization to attract the customers/clients you want, and to build the career you want in dentistry.

Hire to Inspire

If we're never talking about those core/governing values, we're not allowed to hold each other accountable. I'm not suggesting we create contention in an office through a team meeting, calling people out about how that conflicted with, or didn't measure up to, or was inconsistent with, our core/governing values There's no place in an organization for contention.

Everything can be done with respect for dignity. If you just noticed, when people talk, they reveal their values. We just revealed one of ours: You can accomplish everything you need to grow an organization by saying what needs to be said, by holding people accountable without ever robbing an employee of their personal dignity by reprimanding them in public.

We always praise in public and reprimand in private. There's actually a big difference. We redirect when someone wants to do better, and would if they knew how; they just need a little coaching on bringing their performance closer to the standard. A reprimand is only appropriate when every measure of redirect has not worked and clearly, the person doesn't share the values that we do or he or she wouldn't consistently be doing it wrong. Too often, leaders ignore the indiscretions until it's so bad that we have to reprimand. If someone's values are consistent with ours, all anyone needs is a little redirect: let's see if this would be a better approach. And if someone shares your values, they'll lock onto that and the redirection will allow you to move forward in the same direction.

See, we just shared another core/ governing value. That's what we believe a healthy organization that is committed to the same values, should be able to do: hold each other accountable without calling each other out and creating contention within the organization. Now you can see how defined governing values in an organization allow people to grow and to improve their performance.

Lead by example. Your VTI portal is an excellent place where team members can build office systems and protocol along with exploring examples of "how-to" and training. Assign one team member one aspect that he or she can train the team on. Consider doing this exercise once a week and rotate the trainer in your office, giving each team member the opportunity to direct the team to the office system, protocol, marketing promotion, or new technology that has been adopted in your office.

Hire to Inspire

BIOGRAPHIES

Joseph A. Stith, DHK

Joseph's leadership skills were forged in the Unites States Marine Corps. Before his tour ended, he was an award-winning drill instructor training recruits. In 1984 he took these skills with his passion for team building into the private sector to help doctors and dentists create exceptional high-performance work teams. The results they generated were responsible for catapulting their practices into exceptional levels of patient care and financial success. Today, Joseph is the Director of Business Development and Product Engagement at Solutionreach, training consultants and key opinion leaders on advanced technology solutions in healthcare. Call Joseph at 801.201.6357 to schedule a free consultation and learn more.

Bob Leonard

Bob Leonard has a passion for creating successful business and leadership transformations. As a managing partner for Fortune Management, he brings 35 years of leadership, creative problem-solving, team-building and coaching experience to dental practices in the San Francisco Bay Area north of the Golden Gate in Marin, Sonoma and Napa counties. Prior to joining Fortune Management, Bob mastered the art of executive coaching while working as a Group Chairman with Vistage International (the world's leading chief executive membership organization). In this role, he helped numerous CEOs and key executives in various industries achieve positive, lasting growth both personally and professionally.

Before becoming an executive coach, Bob spent 25 years as an advertising executive helping Fortune 500 companies achieve their strategic business objectives. He is a former Vice President with the J. Walter Thompson Company - one of the largest and most respected advertising agencies in the world. His corporate business experience also included working as a marketing executive for Mercedes-Benz USA, where he managed all regional dealership advertising, direct marketing, database marketing and telemarketing in the United States. Immediately after graduating from college, Bob served in the armed forces as a U.S. Marine Corps Infantry officer and achieved the rank of Captain. His academic credentials include earning a Master of Arts degree from Pepperdine University's Graduate School of Education and Psychology and a Bachelor of Arts degree in Liberal Arts at Morehead State University.

Chapter 5

Who to Hire, Inspire or Fire, from the Employee Perspective
Conversations with Tonya Lanthier and Desiree Guevara

> *"A small team of A+ players can run circles around a giant team of B and C players."*
> - Steve Jobs

Oftentimes employees know sooner than their leaders which employees are right for the organization. Why is this? What are we missing as leaders? Listening to employees will give leaders advance notice about when to hire, inspire or fire.

In this chapter, Tonya Lanthier and Desiree Guevara provide us the A-level employees' perspective on what working on a team with B-level and C-level employees does to team productivity and morale. Tonya Lanthier is a registered dental hygienist who has worked in over 100 dental offices and is the founder of DentalPost, the premier online and mobile dental job board for employers and job seekers. Her vast team member experience helps dentists match the right candidate to the right team. Desiree Guevara is a registered dental assistant, clinical instructor and practice management coach at Fortune Management. The team member perspective is very important and adds information that could influence the leader's viewpoint.

First, let's remember that there is no such thing as a perfect employee or a perfect human being. We all have our strengths and weaknesses. It is important to come from the belief that people generally have good intentions and to only question behaviors. In selecting team members, recognize people do have different talents, tools and perspectives based on their past experiences that will shape how they respond and contribute to a given scenario. Certainly, the performance of an individual employee is going to be unique to the makeup of the team and to team dynamics. However, a huge factor in performance is how the individual's personal core values and life vision match with the company core values and vision. So much of an individual's performance is influenced by their character and the amount of passion they have for their work. But none of this will matter if leaders and co-workers are not

41

consistently contributing to outcomes without bias or favoritism.

To complicate things further, it's both good and bad that employees are not forever categorized as A-, B- or C-level. This is why a candidate's references cannot predict future performance. Let's clearly define A-level, B-level and C-level employees:

A-Level employees- are individual contributors who see themselves as partners in your company, not just employees. They usually use words like "we can" and "I will." They are self-motivated; embrace the company vision as their own personal mission; are problem-solvers and decisive; prioritize their work; take ownership over their actions; and volunteer to support co-workers. A-level employees are the best in their respective fields, take initiative and bring new ideas to the table, and are confident that they will perform well, regardless of the circumstances. They know that their level of performance is primarily dependent on what results they accomplish and is only slightly related to external factors. They do not fear other high-ability people, and actually seem to enjoy winning against high-quality competition. In fact, most A-level performers measure the quality of their company by the number of other A-level people the company manages to attract and keep.

When A-level leaders participate in the hiring process, they prefer and seek to hire other A-level employees. There is virtually no fear of competition. In fact, most of these managers understand that hiring top-quality people is the key to their future success, and so will make it easier for those employees to move up in the company. They want to hire people who are winners, just like they are. Desiree Guevara adds, "Being an A-level employee means continuously giving your ultimate best; being a positive and effective team member; never limiting yourself or your responsibilities to your job title."

B-Level employees- generally make up the majority of our workforce. They are competent, solid performers, but are not nearly as engaged or committed to the outcome or vision of the company as A-level performers. B-level employees do not see themselves as partners, nor are they as dedicated to the vision of the company, because they have not embraced it as their own personal mission. Generally they show up ready to work, perform what is expected of them and don't necessarily offer more, because they see the work as merely a job, a means to an end, "a.k.a., a paycheck." Therefore, B-level employees' job satisfaction is contingent on moment-by-moment experiences, external factors. B-level employees are missing that next level of internal drive and passion that A-level employees have, known as a higher purpose.

Hire to Inspire

B-level employees are not generally as confident as A-level employees and can feel threatened by them. They are not as likely to take the initiative and generally do only what is asked of them. The good news is, however, with conscientious development, B-level employees can become consistent A-level performers. The real problem comes when B-level employees are put into the position of being hiring managers. Since they are not overly confident in their ability to perform, especially against A-level co-workers, B-level managers subconsciously hire C-level employees to avoid competition.

Having a team of B-level employees will not provide a low-stress work environment, nor will it be a sustainably self-driving, happy work environment, because there is no higher purpose to the work. And the work can be very good, but not great, without having engaged partners driving the company's success.

C-Level employees- We all know C-level employees. At their best, they are marginally competent, only doing enough not to be fired. They do not have passion for the company vision; for them, it's only a paycheck. They are time-clock watchers and do not participate in team-building activities or support the company event unless they are being paid to do so. They are not partners in the success of the team. You'll hear C-level employees complain more and say "I can't" or "It won't work." It's all about them individually, not the team, and certainly not the company.

Unfortunately, they are not easy to spot when they are being interviewed, because references are not likely to label them as C-level performers, and as candidates, they "put their best foot forward." They are, however, easy to identify after a relatively short period on the job. Their performance is typically mediocre, with a track record of letting their co-workers down. They are full of excuses. C-level employees frequently attribute their lack of success to external factors, taking no personal ownership because "it was outside my control."

Unfortunately, no one wears a sign saying "A," "B," or "C," so the only way to recognize them is to see their work ethic in action and monitor their results. Leaders and their team must hold a strong line of not accepting excuses, only results. Leaders must remain committed to upgrading employees to A-level by setting high standards and consistently monitoring and listening to their team about how tasks are getting done. It's not enough just to know a task is done; leaders must know how it was done and, more importantly, the level of individual participation that went into completing each team task. Are a few

A-level employees completing the group tasks? Ask them what they would do to improve group performance. Have the courage to act on your observations and on their advice, or risk losing your A-level performers. Many successful leaders use the formula of hiring slowly, inspiring consistently and firing quickly to maintain A-level team performance.

Just because you hire an A-level employee doesn't mean they will stay there. A-level employees can easily become B-level performers if the leadership is not reinforcing A-level team dynamics. To be a leader of A-level employees, Tonya and Desiree agree that leaders must walk their talk, which means they must communicate clearly and effectively and act accordingly. Leaders of A-level teams continually take ownership of all the problems and give credit and praise to their team for all the wins. These leaders have the courage and compassion to deliver constructive criticism gracefully, even under pressure, and if necessary, will invite people to leave the team. They make themselves available and listen to their team, providing support when necessary, are passionate about their vision and show the necessary emotional conviction to realize their vision.

In order for leaders to maintain or obtain a team of A-level employees, all team members need to believe in the same vision and to protect the culture of the organization. The entire team must have good communication skills, speak clearly and show respect for one another. A-level teams trust, support and appreciate each other. They apologize and own their mistakes and misunderstandings. A-level teams want to serve a great purpose and feel good about what they do. They will encourage and support coworkers in learning a new skill or taking on a new task. They will acknowledge and thank their teammates for a job well done.

Hiring A-Level Employees

Finding A-level employees is often like finding a needle in a haystack. Who is the right person for your unique culture? Vision? Team? These are loaded questions, filled with many "if this, then that" responses, making it a really tough decision to know who is the best candidate to meet your specific needs. If only leaders had a magic wand or could see into the future, right? The universal advice leaders give is to "hire slowly," because adding a new personality into your team changes the culture, everyone and everything -- hopefully, for the better. Ultimately, the hiring objective is to realize the company vision and to maintain or improve the culture in the process. Having a highly productive team whose knowledge, skills and culture are completely in sync as a functioning unit that creates sustainable company success is the desired outcome.

The hiring process is complicated, because there are so many ways to be off on your decision, and your assessment of who the person really is, versus who he or she is pretending to be during the interview process. Matchmaking the right person's personality, commitment and skill set to the company's culture, vision and team personalities often seems like it simply boils down to instinct and listening to your gut.

But perhaps there's a better way to get more information, using metrics to support your decision. Tonya has written a blog post on her DentalPost website entitled, "Using Metrics to Be More Successful with Your Hiring." In this post she recommends using Personality and Culture Tests, along with Skill and Value Assessments, to support leaders in going beyond that gut instinct. It begins first with understanding what your company culture currently is and deciding if you are happy with it. Are you looking to change the culture with this new hire? If so, what kind of person will it take? With a clearly defined ideal company culture, the next step is to define the person who would be an ideal match for the culture you have or want. Metrics can help you answer this question by looking at the candidate's personality and work style.

Personality and Culture Testing- One popular personality test that we recommend is called the DiSC Model. This personality test has proven to be supportive in matching the right person to the right job with the right team that will support productivity and growth. Essentially DiSC will help leaders understand behavior, temperament and personality, which will reveal compatibility within employee interactions. DiSC is an acronym that stands for:

- D- Dominance measures how an employee will overcome opposition to accomplish results.
- i- Influence measures how a person will shape their environments by influencing others.
- S- Steady tells employers how well an employee will cooperate with others in teamwork.
- C- Compliance evaluates how well an employee will relate to structure.

Culture testing is a metric used more commonly because it helps leaders clearly identify whether a candidate will thrive in the organization's culture. Utilizing this test, leaders examine values, beliefs, outlook and behavioral fit to see if candidates meet their cultural criteria. The cultural test can examine how a candidate will approach a variety of work situations and if their style and behavior match that of the organization. Culture testing takes into consideration the architecture/atmosphere; work style; opportunities for advancement; and commitment level/hours worked, while answering the following questions:

- Is the environment fun or formal?
- How does everyone dress?
- What work hours are expected of the employees?
- Is there travel required with the job?
- Are there flexible work hours?
- How long do employees normally stay with the company?
- What happens when people do not perform well?
- How are people rewarded and acknowledged?
- What type of employee performs best in your company, team players or individual contributors?
- What are team meetings like? Action-driven? Complaint-driven? Light-hearted?
- How does work get done? Individually? In a team?
- How do people communicate? Directly? Indirectly? Verbally or via email?
- How are decisions made? Authoritatively? Collaboratively?

The more clearly delineated the culture is, the easier it is for the candidate to determine if this is a good personal fit. Tonya added, "Data from a cultural test would help match, for example, an employee who demonstrates strong teamwork skills with an organization that places high value on teamwork. This same organization would try to stay away from hiring someone who likes to work alone, as this data would indicate that they might not fit well into the culture."

Skill and Value Assessments- Skills assessment tests are offered on many hiring platforms to measure the various skills and abilities that are important to a particular job. When an employer needs to verify a particular skill set, simulation is an excellent way to verify that such skills have been mastered. Having witnessed the skills in action gives employers a more confident hiring decision based on empirical data, which goes beyond a resume or interview.

Value assessments can help an organization measure the core values of applicants to relate them to the values of the employer. The candidate whose values, beliefs, outlook and behavior are congruent with those existing within the current organization is likely to be a good cultural fit. Employees who do not fit within the environment often leave to find a work environment or culture more congruent with their own values and beliefs. Directly asking the candidate what are their highest life values can provide employers with a good value assessment. However, simply asking this question may not be enough, because not many candidates have the answer well-thought-out, so you must ask more probing questions.

The most important hiring advice we can give leaders in selecting team members is to match personal values and life vision to the company's; only hire happy people who are equally as passionate about the job and the company as the owner is. Find out what their dreams are and why they are in this profession. Verify their passion for what they do. Know the values that drive their passion. Look for candidates who admit to their faults and weaknesses. Most importantly, avoid anyone who talks negatively about his or her last position or employer.

The ultimate outcome when hiring is to weed through all the candidates to find the one who will be committed to do whatever it takes to competently perform the necessary tasks; who will grow with the job; who is compatible with the team personalities and company core values; who has the necessary character to fit on the team; and who finds the compensation mutually beneficial and sustainable for a long employment history.

Inspiring your Team to Become A-Level Employees

This book is about inspiring employees; however, in this section, we are going to tell you what A-level employees want from their leaders. The first thing to know is that inspiring employees is not optional for leaders; it's the daily vitamin employees need to sustain them day-to-day. Another key point is that people are unique, and so, finding out what inspires and motivates them is going to come down to getting to know them better than they know themselves. Desiree and Tonya recommend that leaders give employees purpose by encouraging them to contribute on a leadership level; offering them some control of their environment; supporting them to develop goals; trusting them and not micromanaging them; and encouraging them to think like owners. Employees want to do what is expected of them and want to receive acknowledgement for a job well done. This provides them with purposeful work and gives them a why. It would be hard for anyone to continue to grow and want to do their best if they did not see why their work mattered or how it contributed to the bigger vision of the company.

Taking this further, what is your company's purpose, its contribution to society as a whole? We believe that when leaders frequently remind employees of the company's contribution and their role in making the company vision happen, work becomes more purposeful and meaningful, not just a transaction of time for dollars; it becomes their identity, something they can be proud of. When employees are performing purposeful work, they have a "true north" and know where they are headed; they don't need to be micromanaged because they know how to get where the company wants them to go; and they have earned the trust of the leader, to perform the right tasks for the priority, to complete the mission.

Leaders can inspire outcomes when they stay focused on them, and monitor and measure the results; as the saying goes, "What gets measured gets done." Whenever possible, leaders should look for ways to incentivize results to motivate employee ownership in the outcome. Leaders want employees to think like an owner, be mindful of expenditures and profits, and recognize inefficiencies. A-level employees think like an owner because their work gives them their purpose and they see the company's success as their success. Therefore, A-level employees will push out C-level employees and lift up B-level employees. In order for this to happen, leaders need to actively listen to their A-level employees and recognize that they need to protect their work environment for the success of the company. A-level employees take ownership of what they do when they see their contributions having an effect on the company's success. As Desiree says, "A-level employees see this as their career and will dedicate their skills and talents to innovate for success. A-level employees 'Talk it, walk it, and own it'!"

Leaders must celebrate accomplishments more and reward innovation if they want a team of A-level employees who see themselves as partners. Great leaders will highlight team members' skills and talents and commend them publicly, while privately redirecting and correcting poor performance. Leaders who identify employees' strengths and delegate to their skill set will encourage them to continue to grow, take initiative and become more of an asset to the company. Showing confidence in employees by delegating even more responsibility will inspire more A-level participation in your team. Giving responsibility to employees tells them their leader is confident they can perform the task. Frequent acknowledgment of your team's hard work will motivate them to continue to exceed your expectations.

A-level employees need to be financially intelligent so they can contribute to the bottom line. The more they know about how the company profits and how much it costs to run the business, the more they can support a more profitable company. Ultimately, leaders must rid themselves of mediocrity and encourage entrepreneurial thinking. Initiative and innovation is the goal. Employees know how they can get their job done more efficiently; so the more they know about the finances of their company, the more profits they can deliver. Having a team of dedicated A-level partners engaged in brainstorming "what if" and "is there a better way to reach our goal" thinking makes for a more collaborative and efficient process. They will then think strategically and innovatively about ways to generate revenue, save money and create efficiency.

B- level employees can become A-level employees when they find passion in their work and by:

- Identifying ways to make or save the organization money.
- Proposing a better way of completing a task or process.
- Determining how they can integrate into the company and be more efficient.
- Volunteering to take on a project no one else wants.
- Consistently executing responsibilities through precise follow-up and follow-through.

Leaders must coach A-level employees for retention, B-level employees for performance, and C-level employees to find their happiness elsewhere.

Firing B-Level and C-Level Employees

In the past, companies would focus workplace reductions on C-level employees; however, this strategy does not instill a team of A-level employees, because allowing B-level employees to function at this level lowers A-level to the B-level status. Leaders seeking an A-level team need to hold the line that B-level engagement is not acceptable. Great leaders only want to have happy, passionate people on their team. Supporting a team of A-level employees means protecting the culture and the values. It would be out of an A-level team's integrity to allow unhappy, disengaged employees to remain on their team. Like the saying goes, "You are only as strong as your weakest link," so allowing B-level or C-level commitment means the team is only a B-level or C-level team.

As we previously discussed, most people are B-level employees. The good news is that B-level employees can easily become A-level employees with a sharpening of their skills, a change in their mindset and an adjustment of their focus. Furthermore, due to differences in objectives, roles and responsibilities, someone who is a B-level employee in one organization might be an A-level employee in another company. It's all about the right fit; perhaps they are simply in the wrong job or at the wrong company. Do their skills and talents match the job they have? If not, then perhaps they need a shift of their job duties. Are their skills useful to the purpose of the company's vision? If so, perhaps they need to be specialized in their job duties to match their talents to support the company's needs. Most importantly, is this job and company their happy place? If not, the compassionate and courageous thing to do is to support the employee to journey out and find another company. If leaders do not act fast by releasing the employee, then recognize that "misery loves company" and your A-level team will shift to a B-level or C-level team overnight. The "cancer" will grow and infect all the other emotionally healthy and happy employees.

Certainly it is good to be a leader who comes from a belief that everyone deserves an opportunity to change and better themselves. In this case, there are several discussions and opportunities for the employee to make changes, and if there is no progression and this is impacting the team so that others are not working to the best of their abilities, it's probably time to let them go. Supporting employees to leave makes the decision to fire someone clear. Truthfully, negativity and mediocrity is like a virus; once it affects one person it starts to infect others. If the virus is quarantined to give someone time to heal and get better, then it won't spread any further.

Don't be afraid to fire an employee. While no one hires a new employee expecting to fire them right away, there are times when it has to happen. It is unpleasant, and best to handle sooner rather than later. It is not fair to employees who are performing well to be carrying the weight of B-level or C-level employees, or to have their energy be drained by negativity. Cutting out an employee who is not working well will restore harmony in the workplace and will send a clear message of the value you place on protecting the culture of your work environment and on high-performing employees.

Letting an employee go is one of the most difficult aspects of running a business. And if you're an employee, getting fired is always a shock, even if you might be expecting it. In either case, it's even more challenging when the team is close-knit, and friendships have developed, either employee-to-employee or leader-to-employee. Nonetheless, the fact remains that to grow a company, you need to be consistent in your systems, constantly examining and improving your team components. It's not enough that an employee does their job well; they must also fit as a member of a team within the company culture and have matching values to remain a sustainable team member.

Going through the process of firing an employee is not to be taken lightly. There are certain checklists that you must perform, prior to and immediately following releasing an employee from your company. Everyone will tell you that documentation is essential for all employee corrections and performance appraisals. It is important to review your plan with your legal representative prior to firing someone. However, here are things to consider in preparing: whenever possible, create a written record of performance issues with dates and specifics, before the termination; be like a reporter, answer the who, why, what, when and where questions, always stating termination as a consequence for every relevant infraction. It is imperative that you always provide a proper termination letter with reasons; show that you understand the laws about Cobra extension; explain how the last paycheck and any remaining wages due will be paid; and reinforce and remind the employee of their confidentiality agreement and ongoing obligations.

Final thoughts for leaders

Leaders must continually self-evaluate if they are indeed "walking their talk," and acting as a role model in everything they say. Actions speak louder than words. Leaders will be respected and followed only if employees feel someone with high integrity is leading them. If a leader says one thing yet does another, employees will interpret that to mean it's acceptable behavior.

Remember to stay looking forward and learn to not keep making the same mistakes over and over again. "When one door closes, another one opens. But often we look so long so regretfully upon the closed door that we fail to see the one that has opened for us" -- Helen Keller. This quote needs to be remembered because in life, leaders want to always be moving forward to better themselves. Life will continue to give you similar challenges until you learn the lessons you need to learn, to be prepared for the next challenge. Also if you keep looking back and with regret, then you'll miss out on something special that awaits, so be courageous and do the right thing at the right time.

 "Who to Hire?" no longer has to be a painful question or a tedious process. With your VTI portal, you have access to job descriptions that double as excellent templates for drafting hiring ads. You can also store your office policies, manuals and protocols that support the hiring methods.

BIOGRAPHIES

Tonya Lanthier is CEO of DentalPost, the leading online and mobile dental industry job board in the country, serving more than 450,000 dental professionals and more than 25,000 dental offices. She began her career as a Registered Dental Hygienist in 1995.

Through extensive networking and temping as a hygienist, Ms. Lanthier saw a void in the dental industry employment and communications. She then created an on-line and mobile job board where dental professional could connect. DentalPost sets itself apart by offering metric testing to increase a better match for employment. Ms. Lanthier is a member of the American Dental Hygienists Association (ADHA), Entrepreneurs Organization (EO) and a volunteer at several charities. She also speaks at dental conferences as well as coachin dental job seekers in their careers.

Desiree Guevara is the executive administrator at Fortune Management, the nation's leading practice management company. Desiree brings more than 18 years' experience in office management, dental assisting and dental education. Desiree had the opportunity to work with some of the best dentists in California and knows what it takes to be a valuable team member. As a dental assisting instructor, she taught the many roles required to create a successful team. She emphasizes her belief, the most important elements of a successful team are leadership, communication, a positive attitude and never losing sight of the company's vision.

Chapter 6

Impeccable Communication; It's Always Showtime
A Conversation with Michael Allosso

"Communication works for those who work at it."
- John Powell

Impeccable communication is a prerequisite for any great leader. Communication is a skill that a great leader must continually hone and sharpen. The quality of communication is intricately tied to the quality of our relationships and our ability to be an influential leader. Without impeccable communication, your organization will spin in circles and not reach its true potential. In this chapter Michael Allosso provides leaders techniques of impeccable communication that are so simple yet very effective for the entire organization. Michael Allosso's theater experience as actor, director, choreographer and speaker gives him the communications expertise to have developed his "You on Your Best Day" brand.

Michael teaches leaders crucial communication techniques that will help the entire organization to better reach their full potential. Additionally, he will elevate our communication skills by teaching us:

- Importance of nonverbal communication, also known as micro-messages.
- Why everyone is always on stage and "It's always ShowTime."
- How to give and receive feedback that supports the growth of our relationships in and out of business.
- How engaging your impeccable communication skills will support you in hiring.

Why is Clear Communication So Important?

The number one reason why people leave their professions in America is, they don't feel valued by their boss. Michael says from his experience, "it's not geography, it's not money, it's not the job description. It's that they don't feel valued. The irony is that many bosses do value their employees." The employees don't know they are valued because it hasn't been effectively communicated to them. Leaders don't often take the time to express their gratitude for the skills, talent, dedication and contributions their employees make in their organization. It's not just about a paycheck with employees. In order for the relationship to be sustainable they must feel as if their contributions make a difference. Seventy-one percent of American workers are not engaged in their work because they do not feel passionately connected to their company, co-workers or leaders. What sparks their passion? When Gallup Poll surveyed what would spark employee engagement, workers listed:

25%- Greater clarity about what the organization needs me to do and why

23%- Development opportunities and training

14%- Regular, specific feedback about job performance

10%- Better relationship with co-workers

7%- Better communication with manager

6%- Coach or mentor other than the manager

Reviewing this list it is clear how impeccable communication can ignite passion in employees, since most everything on the list is solved by improved communication. In fact, when Westminster College asked American employees to indicate which incentives would inspire performance, 32% said boosting morale, 27% wanted praise/recognition and only 18% requested monetary awards. Clearly, it's not about the money. Money fails to incentivize employees because it's perceived as part of the employee's compensation package and has no "trophy value," because employees feel awkward discussing this kind of award with others.

Impeccable communication is the leader's "salvation" because it can maintain their employees and keep them engaged. The reality is every word that we say and every movement we make is measured and quantified by the people around us. Therefore it is critical that we take it seriously and practice impeccability with our words and nonverbal communication. People are receiving messages that may or may not be communicating what we want said. Misinterpretations cause people to feel unappreciated, which can lead to their leaving our organization, or worse, they become disengaged Disengaged employees who are unhappy and unproductive typically drain the energy out of the rest of the team. Simply put, without strong communication, we will lose the best people and will create an unhappy culture. This environment is drudgery. People will go to work to punch a clock, not to contribute.

Micro-messages

Equally critical to verbal communication is nonverbal communication or what Michael refers to as "micro-messages." Micro-messages are more than your body language. Micro-messages are everything from your ability to lean forward at a table in a meeting; the car you drive when you pull into the parking lot; and at what speed you pull into the driveway. It's your facial hair; your hairdo; your jewelry; the style of your clothes; the amount of makeup you wear. It's where you choose to live; the décor of your home or business.

Micro-messages are the manners you have, calling people by name, not calling people by name, looking people in the eye, not looking people in the eye, multitasking when someone comes into your office to say hello to you. The list is huge and as you can see micro-messages can change the conversation and the meaning people will link to it. Just as the saying goes, "a picture is worth a thousand words," micro-messages can provide an entire conversation without a single word being said.

Micro-messages are small, unspoken and unconscious messages that are sent and received many times a day. These messages can often be misinterpreted. They can be positive or negative. People create micro-messages at a very fast rate of 10 to 40 micro-messages every ten minutes.

Cultures can be destroyed by these unconscious conversations that are misinterpreted by the subtle things we do or not do. Worse, these messages can accumulate and affect employee productivity, morale, absenteeism, and turnover. Michael's training, "You On Your Best Day" coaching, provides perspective for business leaders and employees to become more conscious of their micro-messages. People who have taken micro-message training say that it changes their behavior immediately. They become aware of their negative messages , stop sending them and concentrate on sending positive messages.

Feedback

As we have already shown, feedback is imperative to supporting the growth and the motivation of your team. They need to have the nourishment that feedback gives them to recharge. "Think about the word feedback for a second. It's a compound word, and what's the first word in feedback? Feed.

So when you give feedback, you are actually nurturing the people around you." You are giving them sustenance. Michael's specific process for giving feedback is called "tsp" or "truthful, specific, positive feedback." "We all know tsp in a simple recipe means teaspoon. So, I believe that feedback is designed to nurture and feed people." Therefore, it's vital to provide nourishment on a daily basis. Feedback is only nutritious if you to give all three ingredients: truthful, specific, positive feedback. It's a triumvirate; you can't just do one of the three to be successful." Michael would not suggest for example that you just give only positive feedback; "Oh, you're wonderful. You're terrific. I love you. You're always so good." This is positive feedback, but the recipient is not going to receive it well. It might even be truthful positive but without the specificity it doesn't have the substance. "The 's' is the critical part of giving feedback." Without the specificity, it lacks the wallop. "You have to be lawyerly in your feedback."

Some teachers and coaches give all positive feedback and it lacks the effective drive to make an impact. The only way to provide "tsp" is to gather information by listening and observing, which requires that you be totally present and aligned with the organization's vision and outcomes. Leaders need to be fully present and fully engaged at all times, observing others looking for specific examples to be able to give "tsp." As Michael says, a great leader is like a great parent "gathering beauty constantly." So if you're a beauty gatherer you're getting all this data, and then you're sending the data out. The beauty of giving truthful positive feedback is that it will mean more to the recipient. Obviously, this is going to encourage more of that behavior and employees now know what a good job looks like. People *are* going to go home feeling more self-confident, validated and appreciated. When leaders feed their employees with "tsp," employees can take that positive energy home and have energy to share with their family. Ultimately, it is common practice to tell employees to leave their domestic problems at home when they come to work, but shouldn't they also be able to leave work with all their energy loops closed? Yet another benefit is when employees are getting enough "tsp," they will be able to hear your more critical feedback. In fact, they will welcome your criticism because they want to please you and receive more "tsp," because you have established a relationship of "honoring their beauty."

Criticism is a necessary and important part of learning and growing. It's important for leaders to support an environment whereby failures lead to learning. Sandwiching negative criticism between positive feedback cannot be the only time that employees receive feedback. Sandwiching in criticism is when leaders start with "tsp," fill in the criticism and end it with "tsp." Michael is not opposed to the sandwich technique, especially in performance evaluations, as long as employees are receiving "tsp" at other times. Otherwise when positive feedback is given, the recipient will be waiting for the other shoe to drop. The problem with this approach is the employee never really hears the positive feedback. Leaders have to individually read their employees to know how much "tsp" versus criticism they can share successfully to maintain growth and engagement. As Michael put it, "What's the point of giving direct critical feedback if the person isn't going to receive it and do something with it?" To illustrate this point, Michael tells the story of how he approaches this when he is directing a play, "I pretty much give nothing but 'tsp,' straight-up observations that are positive on the first few days of rehearsal. Then on the fourth day of rehearsal, people are lining up saying, 'Michael what should we do here, how can we make this scene better?' When leaders feed them with great specificity and see excellence in others, employees will trust and respect the leader's opinion. "Employees not only are willing to hear your criticism, but they will seek you out for it. They're eager for the collaboration of how they can get better."

The key is to build a culture of leaders leading leaders within your organization *and* for the team to provide "tsp" to each other as well. When colleagues are acknowledging each other, spreading the beauty around the office, the culture will be supportive, collaborative and encouraging. This will lead to more creativity, innovation and increased productivity. The people within the organization will want to take risks and want to achieve because they know it will be recognized. "Everybody appreciates being recognized for what they did well by someone they respect and value. Don't be fooled by people who say they don't need that."

It's Showtime!

'It's Showtime!' has been a major part of Michael's life from the beginning of his career. Majoring in theater arts, Michael spent the first ten years of his career as a high school drama teacher nurturing and feeding teenagers to perform excellence. He credits the time he spent with them as being the most profound time of embracing 'It's Showtime.' At the core of his teaching, he modeled impeccably being in the moment, and being focused and committed to excellence. This led him to the career of coaching executives and speaking today. "I learned a lot about myself in those ten years; for instance, if you believe in someone, the magic it creates in their soul and in their mind to create things they didn't even know they could do is incredible. What I taught them most perhaps was self-confidence, and the road to self-confidence." The key to "It's Showtime" is focus and concentration

During those ten years, Michael recalls two events in his personal life that challenged him to stay in "It's Showtime" mode. He got divorced and his dad died. Being Catholic, he grew up with the belief "you get married for life." Equally shocking, Michael's dad was a strong fireman who was never sick a day in his life. He was diagnosed with cancer and died a year and a half later. Both events occurred within six months of each other while he was teaching high school. Michael was devastated; family is so important to him. Interestingly, Michael noticed his high school students got better during that time because he was even more committed to his passion. He was not going to let his focus and concentration suffer. you could make a million excuses why you should stop reading this book. "You have a headache. Somebody needs you. You have a physical ailment, spiritual ailments, work problems, family problems. We all have them. They are all real." The idea of 'It's Showtime' is, nobody cares what problems you have. "It's not that people aren't compassionate or empathetic. It's just that if you show up and you choose to show up, 'It's Showtime.'

'It's Showtime' means playing full out, being on and engaged with the people who surround you, and being totally dialed into your micro-messaging. Let's say something is causing you stress that you cannot deal with. Stay home or "do what Steve Martin did on the set of *Pink Panther 2*; go into your trailer and close the door." *Pink Panther 2* is a movie that Michael had the great fortune of working on. The original example of the "It's Showtime" phrase comes from the great Bob Fosse in the movie *All That Jazz* with Roy Scheider. "Roy Scheider plays Bob Fosse, the great theatrical director and choreographer. Fosse was a genius, but had a little trouble in his personal life. He was a womanizer, alcoholic and chemical abuser. So when his alarm clock went off in the morning, it was tough for him to get going. He would drag his sorry butt out of the bed, get into the bathroom and look himself in the mirror, and say, 'It's Showtime.' Sometimes this might be what it takes for you too. 'It's Showtime' means you've got to bring it with great energy and passion.

"Energy creates more energy. Lethargy creates lethargy." So you bring that energy level to the workplace on a daily basis.

'It's Showtime' is how Michael feels many opportunities come into place. In fact, when you focus and stay connected, giving off the proper micro-messages, you have the wherewithal to seize opportunities that might otherwise pass you by. Michael attributes his successful coaching career to the utilization of his "It's Showtime" philosophy. While conducting a high school rehearsal, an observant parent made the connection that this style would work with CEO's.

His coaching has developed into a huge client base that encompasses forty-three of the fifty states as well as Canada, the United Kingdom, and Ireland. A sampling of his client base includes the fields of construction, insurance and media services. There is no limit to the categories of businesses and services that profit from Michael's training.

Michael emphasizes the end of the day is when you put your head on the pillow to go to sleep, not when you get home and walk in the door. Your family deserves the same focus and concentration that you bring to your work day.

Connection with family is incredibly important. Both "tsp" and "It's Showtime" are as necessary parts of a rich family life as they are in business. Most of us would say that we value family life above all else. How incredible would it be to bring the most energy and love you have to those you love most? Wow, how powerful would this be?

One of the most important things you can do to make the mental shift of staying in the moment is to take a breath.

Ask yourself, what is the breath you need to take literally, and *what's a breath you need to take figuratively? Where and when you* do need to go into your trailer and close your door like Steve Martin? When you do need to go take a walk by yourself so you can get back into "It's Showtime"? Breathing gives everyone a moment to pause. The pause allows us to process the moment, to focus and to make sure your message is being heard. Listening and observing in the pause cues you to your surroundings. What is the energy around you?

Is the person you are speaking to in a state to listen?

Some very simple things can enhance your ability to engage a person's attention.

Do you look people in the eye when speaking to them? Eye contact is a must.

I would say a sense of humor is paramount. Is there enough humor in your workplace and at home? Humor can enhance an environment. Humor must be appropriate, not sarcastic and not at someone else's expense.

"You on Your Best Day" starts with looking in the mirror before you leave in the morning and saying, "Yeah, I look great today." This will help you to perform better and sustain the energy required to be totally "on" from the beginning to the end of your entire day.

So how do you look great and feel great? Take a look introspectively at how you are showing up every day. Are you doing things that create energy and support you to look your best? What are you eating? Are you exercising? What are you wearing? How do you look? You're going to a show. What's the right costume for the show? What's going to make your performance better?

William Ball, in his wonderful book, *A Sense Of Direction*,[15] talks about how structure frees creativity. "You on Your Best Day" entails that we go all day with "sterling preparation blended with the utmost spontaneity."

It's the structure of being prepared for your role that leverages opportunities for creativity to emerge throughout the day's performance. Have a very structured objective of what you want to accomplish in a day. This allows you to deal with obstacles you might face along your way. Having that structure frees you to be creative all day long, to see the beauty surrounding you. "So, if you're good at winging it at meetings, try backing it up with some structure. Have a strong beginning, have a strong end in all your interactions. Have a story that you know you're going to tell." Structure is going to liberate you to be creative, and that's how you'll go through the day in this show-time mode. One structure recommendation Michael has is to begin and end each calendar day with something non-work-related. "Do something for you. Don't go to bed checking the emails and writing a memo. Don't wake up and run to your computer or make a business call. Instead sing a song, take a walk or make love. It's just going to make you a much better leader and human being."

Heightening the Stakes

Heightening the stakes means you make every moment in your life the most important. Every moment counts! So if you bumped into a client at Starbucks on Saturday afternoon, you keep your stakes high. Can you be profane and inappropriate at that meeting because it's not Monday through

Friday and you're not on the clock? Parents: are you off the clock if your child wakes you up at 3 a.m.?

It's exhausting to heighten your stakes, but three things happen when you do: 1) excellence 2) repeat business. Someone may not need what you have to offer when you meet them. But if your stakes are high, they remember you. 3) You sleep beautifully at night. Making every moment important gives you higher purpose. What if you said, 'I want this human being to be better after having interacted with me? What if this happened at every single interaction, even if you're firing somebody? Can you imagine how excellent all these communications would be?"

Hiring

Don't hire people who are like you; that could be the kiss of death. The key to hiring is diversity in all skill sets and personalities; keep the variety.

- Look for people who have common values, core values, aspire to the culture.
- Try interviewing candidates outside the work environment, like at a restaurant. Michael recommends this: "I watch how people treat folks like waiters and bus people. Watch how those people are treated. If the candidate treats those people with dignity and respect, this candidate might be a keeper. If they don't respect other people, I don't think you want them there."
- Be suspicious of candidates who are trying to just suck up to get the job. Look for a real person, one who respects other people
- Caution with team members interviewing candidates. No matter what, the buck stops with the leader. Sometimes when you give people the opportunity, they think that means, "I've got to find out what's wrong with the candidate." The bottom-line is leaders need to weigh all the advice, and make sure the final decision is theirs. Michael says,"I welcome the collaboration, I love the collaboration. I often will bring someone with me to casting whose eye I trust. As long they understand I have the final say.
- Look for candidates with impeccable focus and concentration during the interview, who come highly prepared and demonstrate poise and confidence. Look for people whose body language is inclusive and enthusiastic."

Hire to Inspire

Michael's Favorite Interview Questions:

- Is there anything not on your resume, you think I should know about you that you'd like to tell me? This is a great question to open the interview with.
- Is there anything about yourself that my questions haven't afforded you the opportunity to say about yourself that you'd like me to know? This is a great question to ask at the end.
- What they're most proud of in their life?
- What's the ideal boss for you?

 In your VTI portal video store you have access to a number of videos by talent such as Michael Allosso and others who present excellent training around mastering communication skills, and subjects such as "how to say it better," the emotional triggers, understanding benefit statements, and how to get and stay in rapport with your patients. An all-star training team at your fingertips.

BIOGRAPHY

Michael Allosso's theater experience as actor, director, choreographer and speaker gave him the communications expertise to develop his "You on Your Best Day" brand. He presents motivational and job performance seminars to companies seeking to help their CEOs and employees to better reach their full potential. Allosso is a Vistage speaker and has presented at hundreds of Vistage CEO meetings. He practices what he preaches—in other words, he is a great communicator. He speaks in sound bites, he speaks clearly and his information could be crucial to your success. He is the master in observing the people. He tells leaders what he sees going on with the people in their organization through his casting director experience. Leaders are told how their people come across to the average citizen. "I'm looking at everybody as a potential casting candidate. So they walk in my casting door, and I'm going to give you how they come across."

Chapter 7

Embracing Change for Growth- C.A.N.I.®
A Conversation with Shannon Richkowski

"Change is inevitable, progress is not. No matter how much we try to fight it, things are going to change in our lives. Progress, however, is the result of conscious choice."
- Tony Robbins

Life in and out of business is consistent in that change is inevitable. Learning how to embrace change is a necessary life skill for us all to master. Change is simply a transformational process of growth, best experienced when you envision it, initiate it, and control it. Converting change into a transformational process supports feelings of curiosity and an openness to ask, "What is this life lesson going to teach me?" When change is embraced as character-building moments to grow and learn from, they are less scary and perhaps even exciting. Seeing change as a transformational process allows for a more peaceful acceptance. Resisting change causes drama, builds fear and worry ("negative goal setting"). Negative goal setting means telling your brain something negative is going to happen and making it happen. Acknowledging change allows it to happen and unfold. Embracing change allows you to plan ahead for numerous scenarios versus sticking your head in the sand hoping nothing bad will happen.

Adjusting your expectations will support you in embracing change. Reducing expectations means that you don't expect or demand certain results; you accept that nothing lasts forever; and you live in the now. Unreasonable expectations of life will be met with disappointment and resentment.

Seeing everything in life as a gift and as an opportunity for a C.A.N.I. [®6] (constant and never-ending improvement) moment means change is met freely. As the saying goes, "The pain is in the resistance." Shannon Richkowski is a leader who is passionate about this message. She is the

63

perfect model of C.A.N.I.®6. as a coach for Fortune Practice Management and the director of Hygiene Mastery, where she encourages her coaches to be designers of change rather than to live in the aftereffect of change. Shannon supports leaders in embracing change by consciously choosing to play a role in how the change is unfolding. Her goals:

- Help leaders learn how important embracing change is to growing an organization and its people.
- Describe why leaders must embrace change for themselves and adopt a culture of C.A.N.I. ® throughout their organization.
- Support leaders in encouraging employees to embrace change and growth, avoiding resistance at every turn and an "uphill battle" from the people in their organization.
- Explain how C.A.N.I. ® prevents people from being a barrier to their own success.
- Provide support with hiring and interview techniques that will reveal candidates' willingness to embrace change and contribute in a culture of C.A.N.I. ®

Embracing Change For Organizational Growth

As we have said, change is going to happen whether you want it to or not, but progress is optional. Life's lessons will keep repeating until we have absorbed the lesson fully. In life and in nature, if organisms are not growing they are dying; the same is true with organizations. Organizations create sustainable growth by growing their people, who can only grow when they fully embrace change. The lack of growth for team members is similar to what we see in children: idle time. When children have idle time on their hands, it leads to boredom. Most people replace boredom with non-productive actions, which in turn lead to poor outcomes such as gossiping or finding ways to create drama. Being given an opportunity to have personal growth in an organization is the most valuable gift a leader can give a team member. It also happens to be the best investment to make in an organization.

Fortune Practice Management says, "Grow your people, grow your practice." Team members who are given opportunities for professional and personal growth are inspired, connected and eager to contribute. Business owners need to recognize that it's not all about the money in dealing with employees. Employees want growth. Giving a valued unhappy team member a raise is not going to fix the situation entirely. The problem with the raise is, even though it may be warranted, it's only half of the story. No money could ever replace the beauty of being fulfilled with inspiration, being challenged, or having the opportunity to contribute.

Embracing change has two steps. The first step is recognizing we have a choice, and both choices have their consequences. The second step is making the distinction of what embracing change looks like when you are in total alignment with it. Once we have embraced the change, we can start working through the obstacles rather than being stuck in them. We will see resources and opportunities that we had not seen before. We will effect change rather than change happening to us. Our choice in addressing change will have a direct impact on the quality of our personal and professional life.

When change is embraced as growth and you can see that failures lead to learning, you inevitably grow stronger. The ability to continuously accept change allows you to become as solid as a rock, even if you feel afraid. Learning to accept change as a part of life fills you with calmness, peace, and courage. Courage, since you have references from the past of all the change you have endured and so you realize that change can't break you. The more you permit change and impermanence, the more you will grow as a person. When we can accept change, learn from it, and become all the better for experiencing it, change is no longer our enemy. It becomes our teacher.

Creating an environment that embraces change and C.A.N.I.®

When it comes to creating an environment that embraces change and supports a C.A.N.I.® culture, leaders need to align themselves with employees who support such a cause. A single leader alone cannot create the culture. The leader does, however, get to decide who they will have on their team. When leaders find employees who share their beliefs and help communicate these beliefs, there are no boundaries to what they can accomplish together. Employees need to know why change is necessary and how change brings them closer to the vision.

Leaders must align supporters with their cause by creating emotional attachment to outcomes. Otherwise an organization will have one leader in front of a room saying, "This is what's going to happen, and this is what is going to get done." Such an approach will not support the growth of the organization or its people. The more people supporting the change, the less resistance will be met and the more likely the desired effect will be achieved. This is best accomplished by coaching employees to be leaders leading leaders. We will dive deeper into this subject in Chapter Ten, Participatory Ownership.

Leaders leading leaders within the company need to be emotionally attached to the outcome, which happens by knowing how and where the organization is heading, why this is important, how it will it move us closer to what we all want, and finally, what's in it for me, personally. When team members believe that change is going to bring the entire team closer to the vision, then the effort it will take or the learning curves they'll have to endure, all become worth it. As leaders, we must create an environment that allows open and honest communication. Changes big or small have fears and struggles to accompany them. The environment must be safe to discuss those fears and struggles so that they can be worked through by masterminding.

Masterminding that supports leaders leading leaders, C.A.N.I.® and embracing change, gives the entire team a voice to offer solutions on issues. When you and your team commit to C.A.N.I.®, anything is possible and there are no boundaries or limits. Goals are achieved and standards are raised. Shannon Richkowski says C.A.N.I.® provides "an opportunity to live my life to its fullest and not letting life just happen to me. I get to be the creator of my own destiny. Within our organization, our entire philosophy is built on C.A.N.I.®. It's a must."

Leaders' Role in C.A.N.I.®

In creating an environment of C.A.N.I.®, it's important for leaders to be selective in choosing their team. Every person has his or her specific roles and contributions to make. When leaders realize that they have people who are not committed to C.A.N.I.®, it is critical they protect the environment by giving the person the freedom to go. Protecting the culture of C.A.N.I.® is the responsibility of the leader and as Richkowski says, "If I'm keeping somebody in my business who is not right, that's hindering the employee from being fulfilled. That is going to be upsetting for them and oftentimes for the people around them." Leaders must have the courage to say, this person is not a good fit.

She relates a quote by Carl Jung about leadership: "Children are educated by what the grown-up is, not by his talk." "I love that because as leaders, we can say that we're going to master culture but we must master it before we can request others to take it on." Leaders must also be willing to speak up when they see behaviors or actions that do not represent the C.A.N.I.® culture.

To inspire employees to learn and engage, leaders need to hold employees and themselves accountable. A great accountability tool we recommend to leaders is the ultimate success formula[7] by Anthony Robbins from his book *Unlimited Power*[16]. This is a four-step process for achieving results. The first step is to know exactly what you want, to be clear about your outcome. It is critical to know why you want this outcome and to know what the consequences will be if the outcome is not realized. The next three steps are "taking massive action," "monitoring your results," and if you're not getting what you want, "changing your approach over and over as many times as it takes." This creates commitment to change.

C.A.N.I.® requires regularly masterminding in areas that we would like to see improvement. Creating repeatable systems through resources such as VTI (Virtual Training Innovations) elevates C.A.N.I.® to a massive scale. Shannon Richkowski cautions leaderd to do less telling and ask more questions. "We tend to tell, tell, tell. We do a lot of talking. As leaders we need to improve our listening skills, and also ask lots of questions." The more questions you ask, the more insight you get, and the more information, which can be priceless. Remember that inspiring others is not about our own personal agenda.

Hiring Advice

Don't be too eager to fill the position. As leaders, we often get too focused on the position and rush to hire people. Regardless of the task, their skills, or their experience, it is most important to find candidates who share your beliefs. Next, identify if they have the skills to fulfill the position. Unfortunately, leaders frequently look for those who have the skills, rather than identifying if they are aligned with your vision and goals.

Interview Questions

- **What does change mean to you?** A candidate's honesty will show, even if they're trying to convince you that they welcome change. The tone of their voice and their body language will give you the sense that they would actually run away from change.

If change excites them, their body language will be congruent. Do they sit up straight with their shoulders back and say, "Wow, change, I welcome it because it motivates me" or do they look scared, as if they are trying to actually convince themselves that they welcome change.

- **What was the last thing that you did that truly pushed you outside your comfort zone?** If they have to think about it and go back 15 years, that is probably a hint that they don't embrace change and tend to stay in their comfort zone.

- **Tell me the last time that you took on learning something new. What was it like? How did it make you feel?** Again, listen to how they explain their answer. They will tell you if they move toward change or try to avoid it at all costs.

- **What does the word failing mean to you?** Listen to find out if they are open to trying new things and to stepping out of their comfort zone. We are listening for anything about learning, or needing to change the way they approach uncomfortable situations.

CANI®- Constant and Never Ending Improvement . . .with this attitude, your office will have the backbone of a practice that adapts to change. Your VTI portal will act as the vehicle that drives all of your team and their departments to a higher level of efficiency. With over 100 hours of continuing education videos from top business coaches in the world, to foundational documents and monitors for key indicators your practice needs to grow, a CANI® culture is well supported.

BIOGRAPHY

Shannon Richkowski, RDH is the Director of Hygiene Mastery and a coach for Fortune Practice Management. Under her direction, Hygiene Mastery has gained national renown for delivering the kinds of detailed, progressive strategies that enable dental practices to maximize their potential. That this sought-after speaker brings such thoughtful, high-impact analysis to her role should come as no surprise; her astute observations are born of 20 years of industry knowledge as a hygiene educator, dental coach and registered, laser-certified dental hygienist.

Hire to Inspire

In addition to being a member of the American Dental Education Association, Academy of Laser Dentistry and Directory of Dental Speakers, Shannon has honed her consulting skills through advanced training with Fortune Management, Pac-Live, PDA and GenR8TNext. Each nugget of past experience and continuing education—including expertise in business administration—helps to bring the modern-day challenges facing dental teams into sharper focus.

As a result, Shannon and Hygiene Mastery consistently empower practices by successfully identifying and eliminating the obstacles that impede a seamless integration of patient care, clinical excellence and profitability. Her philosophy of "support at a whatever-it-takes level"—buoyed by her thorough understanding of the latest cutting-edge technology for RDHs—is changing the dynamics of hygiene departments across all socioeconomic communities. Along the way, dental professionals around the country are seeing the powerful impact that hygiene teams can have on a practice's big picture and bottom line.

Raising the standards of professional care is more than just a business mantra for this proud military wife. One of Shannon's passion projects involves offering dental care in Nicaragua through Bridges of Hope International, the faith-based nonprofit that provides resources and relief to impoverished people in Central and South America.

Exclusive Gift for You! $2500 Value – A Complimentary Department Analysis & Opportunity Assessment by a Hygiene Mastery Coach

Includes:
- A complimentary Hygiene Department Analysis: uncover great opportunities for your hygiene department through a comprehensive evaluation focusing on HM's 5 Pillars of a Comprehensive Hygiene Department.
- A conference call identifying areas of strength and areas that present missed opportunities • A one-hour follow-up call to discuss one topic of your choice • A Periodontal Percentage Calculator, a tool that measures success and points you to ways to improve your Periodontal Program.

**To redeem, email: hygiene@hygienemastery.com
Or call (866) 520-0127 to schedule your appointment.**

Chapter 8

Developing Talent through Mentoring, Praise and Encouragement
A Conversation with Vicki McManus

"Correction does much, but encouragement does more."
- Johan Wolfgang von Goethe

No matter what kind of organization you run, engaged and happy employees are essential to making it operate successfully. Mentoring, praising and encouraging employees are directly linked to the desirable business outcomes of productivity, customer service, quality, retention, safety and profit. In order to create engagement and happiness you must, as a leader, develop your employees as *talent* and not just cogs in a machine. Employees engaged in their work are more likely to remain committed to their employer, stay focused on achieving business goals, and to drive the organization's future in the right direction.

Shockingly, less than one-third of American employees feel engaged and connected to their company. Why is this? How do leaders create a passionate workforce? Vicki McManus shares ways to mentor, praise, engage and encourage; which statistics say will go much further than monetary incentives. She will in this chapter:

- Persuade leaders to grow their people in order to grow their organization
- Help leaders structure systems for mentoring and inspiring talent growth
- Explain how to provide positive feedback to employees during their talent development
- Share ways to praise, engage and encourage that are meaningful to each employee
- Provide hiring tips and tricks that will find the right people for the team

Vicki McManus has written *the* guide on how to praise and encourage teams in her book: *Fundamentals of Outstanding Dental Teams*[17]. She is the CEO of Productive Dentist Academy, Founder of Neighborhood Smiles LLC and owns her own marketing firm. She is also the author of *Frustration, the Breakfast of Champions*[18]. Vicki says people want to be recognized and do purposeful work and a little acknowledgement goes a long way. If you, as the leader show that you have noticed an employee and are appreciative of their contributions, you will be surprised at the positive outcomes you will gain. She says employees want feedback. Feedback can take many forms, but the most successful types include:

1. Daily coaching and assistance fine-tuning professional skills
2. Consistent recognition of how efforts are making a difference
3. Ongoing review of the vision and core values of the business
4. Acknowledgement of how daily efforts contribute to team success

Feedback is fundamental if leaders want to see their team take pride in daily work. But how is that feedback best given? When is it appropriate and effective? McManus says leaders should:

1. Have frequent 1:1 meetings with employees
2. Provide opportunities to have ongoing informal conversations
3. Make continuing training and development a priority
4. Celebrate the wins and highlight the talent's greatness through incentive programs

It's Not All about the Money

Motivating talent is not all about the money. Believe it or not, connecting with employees in order to see the outcomes you want is easier (and cheaper) than you may think. It may come as a shock, but if you want your team to be happy and engaged start with the basics. Many studies have shown that employees desire the following in their work place:

- Structure
- Job descriptions with clear goals and boundaries about who's accountable for specific tasks
- Clear understanding of who is/are the decision makers
- Clear understanding of the overall the game plan, the rules and their role
- Career developmental opportunities and training
- Regular, specific feedback about job performance

- Improved relationships with their co-workers and leader
- A coach or mentor
- Flexible job conditions

Know your people

1:1 Growth Conferences

If your goal is to build a culture of leaders leading leaders, then a 1:1 Growth Conference is an essential tool to discovering employees' personal interests. Leaders need to know who their employees are as individuals so they can appreciate their specific aptitudes. 1:1 meetings educate leaders about how best to support the professional and personal growth of their team. McManus reminds us, "The people on the front lines know far more about their business than the people sitting in the management suite."

1:1 Growth Conferences provide leaders with invaluable insight about how employees operate. The meetings also provide a space to share valuable information from leadership to the team. Employees should learn what mix of benefits matters most to leadership. Employees can then communicate what skills they wish to acquire as they develop their careers. 1:1 meetings are a discovery process. The leader gets the opportunity to say to employees, "I believe in you and want to support you." A key to 1:1 meetings is creating an atmosphere that is open and welcoming; a safe place where employees have the freedom to share their ideas without fear of being reprimanded.

Employees become business partners when they are given permission to engage in entrepreneurial thinking. Robust organizations are not built on the backs of employees who only do as they are told. Micromanagement is not sustainable for you as a leader and is exhausting for the team. An environment that supports entrepreneurial thought from employees encourages them to become allies that feel personal responsibility to the organizational mission. When leaders create this type of culture, life becomes considerably easier. The leader's role becomes that of coach, continually finding ways to support his or her employees' growth.

1:1 Growth Conference best practices:
- Schedule 30 to 60 minutes of uninterrupted time at least three times a year, e.g., February, May and September.
- Leaders should listen more than talk, asking questions like, "What

do you think?" and, "How do you feel about that?"

- Recognize that transparency is a valuable type of inspiration. The more you're willing to share about the company (overhead, growth, and numbers) the more your employees can engage in your business.
- Come prepared. Require that employees complete the *1:1 Growth Conference Pre-Meeting Surveys* at least one week prior to the meeting so the leader can review them, make notes and create the meeting around critical points.
- Encourage the employee to get the most out of their time with you by asking, "What's most important in todays' meeting for you?"
- The leader should stay focused and engaged in the conversation the entire time. Eliminate distractions. Gifting someone with your full attention has a huge impact on solidifying the impression that you truly care.
- Close the meeting by reviewing the commitments made to include dates for completion of tasks.
- Leaders should take the time directly after the meeting to make notes on the highlights of the meeting and to reflect on them.

Clearly, the days of the carrot-and-stick bonus motivator are long gone. People want to have their work make a difference. They want to continually learn and grow in a coaching relationship with their boss. They're smart, and can Google almost anything to find the answer to any question; so give them what they can't find online: benchmarks and goals. That way they can self-adjust to make a difference. Today's workers are not going to accept a leader saying, *Do this because I asked you to*, and you wouldn't want one who did.

Workers today do not necessarily want to work for the same company for 30 years in hopes of retiring with a gold watch and a great pension. The employee mindset is to learn what he or she can from a job in order to take that experience with them to the next job. While initially counterintuitive, an employee who knows their employer supports their development even if it means eventually leaving the company, will more likely stay with you for the long haul. Additionally, the smart leader knows that even if they move on they can be an asset down the road. Overall, a leader's goal is to develop entrepreneurial thinking so that employees come with ideas and solutions; they are problem-solvers rather than problem-creators.

Ongoing Feedback and Continuous Training

Most employees try to meet expectations and standards. The problem arises when they don't know exactly what you are looking for. The number one success tool for organizations is praise and encouragement. Most employees would say they receive far more negative than positive feedback, which can be a demoralizing experience. Positive reinforcement of behavior you like will encourage repetition of those actions. Praise is a reward available to you at all times, it costs you nothing and never loses its effectiveness.

Praise is a great motivator when it is explicitly linked to an action that supports the overall organization. When praise and encouragement are given, employees get the immediate reward of knowing exactly how their actions led to success. Thus, the organizational goal becomes bigger than the time clock and *that* is what it is all about.

Coaching employees through failure is an integral part of leadership. You must help them understand that failures lead to learning. As Abraham Lincoln said, "My great concern is not whether you have failed, but whether you are content with your failure."

Employees are more innovative and willing to contribute when their leader is optimistic and finds a silver lining in every experience, especially a failure. People need praise and encouragement along the way to success, and good leaders know success does not often happen on the first try. Vicki McManus suggests a four-question Silver Lining Process:

- Where have we already created success, no matter how small? It's important to remind employees, especially new employees, that success takes time.
- What is good about this situation right now?
- How can I change my approach to get better results?
- What support do I need to reach success?

Employee satisfaction surveys are another way leaders show their commitment to creating a happier workplace. The value of a survey is that it quickly gets the answers you need. In a few moments you can find out if employees are happy with their team, their training, your leadership or any other aspect of the job. The results of a workforce questionnaire can give you the data you need to help avoid staff turnover and create a more productive working environment. Surveys are also critical for employees as a safe way to provide peer feedback. When the surveys are read, team members can be coached to be solution-driven with any issue, finding a balance between being encouraging and critical.

Great leaders are mentally prepared and open to receiving criticism themselves. Tony Robbins states, "All communication is either a loving response or a cry for help." Leaders need to be role models when being critiqued. They should respond first by being grateful for the information, because there is no perfect leader or perfect employee; we are all works in progress. A simple system for leader feedback can be a suggestion box in the break room.

Vicki McManus uses the Tiny Pulse digital survey tool. "I love Tiny Pulse because it asks one question a week [or every two weeks] of all the employees. It is designed to measure happiness at work. There is also an area where they can virtually thank other people on the team, 'cheers to peers' as I like to say. The system includes anonymous feedback tools so that management can discover missed opportunities and employees feel safe."

Surveys are only as effective as the questions asked. A few tips from the experts:

- Ask well-crafted questions that are brief and that clearly define your goals
- Use straightforward, supportive language
- Change questions often to get more perspective on different areas
- Keep the questions anonymous whenever possible to get the most honest feedback

We also suggest that the employees answer the Working /Not Working Survey. This survey provides leaders leading leaders with language that supports the employees' commitment to being part of the solution.

Working/Not Working Survey:
- What's working?
- What's not working about_____?
- What changes are you willing to make?
- What options are you considering?
- What support do you need?

The Working/Not Working Survey delivers differing perspectives on issues while also providing employees a voice. It enhances the culture of problem-solving and reduces scapegoating or blaming.

It is true, motivating employee behavior is not all about the money; in fact, it's all about C.A.N.I.® (constant and never-ending improvement) as a necessary engagement tool. Check in with the employees as a group and ask each person, "What resources do you need? What training do you need?" Tell your employees it's important to continually look for areas in which the company, the leadership and the individual worker can succeed. Being sincerely interested in your employees' success and having them recognize you believe in them means so much more than money. Basically, McManus says, "lend them your confidence as they're building their own." Tell them, "That's exactly what I was looking for. How can we take it a little further?" Train them to be leaders, to take the initiative, to be problem-solvers and critical thinkers and you won't have to micromanage another day of your life.

Ask yourself, "What am I doing to demonstrate that I value people in my organization?"

Incentive and Recognition Programs

Incentive programs are set up to reward results and motivate performance. Awards are fuel to ignite self-motivation and encourage growth. When leaders create incentive or recognition programs it is critical to know what individuals are passionate about. Both incentive and recognition programs must be well crafted to both motivate individuals while also achieving the desired team effect. When systems work they convert company values into employee habits. Ideally such programs focus on specific goals that create a culture of excellence, which in turn boosts morale. Increased morale then increases company loyalty, which leads to lasting results. The leader's challenge is to match rewards to both individual and team motivation triggers.

The most ineffective incentives are those that pit people or departments against each other, making them hyper-focused on their area while losing focus on the big-picture needs. Full-team incentives are generally better because they reward everyone for working together to reach a result. Be careful that your incentives coincide with desired business results. Recognition and praise incentives that work can be as simple as naming an employee of the month or employee of the year. The fun part about this is that you can create any award you want. We suggest you actively pursue regional, state and national awards and nominate both individual employees and your company. The best recognition of all is praise from their peers.

Celebrate, Laugh and Make Work Fun!

The number one killer of productivity is stress. If you're not having fun during your day you're not as productive as you could be. As Clint Eastwood says, "Take your work seriously, but don't take yourself seriously." Simply laughing can both lower your stress level and be contagious in making someone's day a bit less stressful.

Fish, [19] a book by Stephen C. Lundin, PhD, Harry Paul, and John Christensen, is a must-read for teams that want to elevate their work experience. The world-famous Pike Place Fish Market in Seattle has an incredible commitment to the service-inspired Fish! Philosophy™. The culture is based on the simple principles of making the day amazing for people around you through play, and staying focused on being of service to others. Incorporating the Fish! Philosophy™ into your organizational culture will motivate customers and talent. New customers and excellent talent will gravitate toward your company because of its positive power. As you put the fun back into your business, assess any negative forces in your company as well. It's okay for employees to be shy or introverted, but don't let negative attitudes drain the life out of your business. As the leader, you must be excited about the prospect of having fun while working. Your enthusiasm will be contagious.

The key theme to morale-boosting activities that work is to make sure people don't feel uncomfortable or disrespected. Remember, you can't force-feed fun to your employees. Some will immediately respond to your cues, while others will need more time. There's nothing worse than mandatory attendance at a company outing because "We're all here to have fun!"

To be meaningful, celebrations must be timely. If you wait too long, it becomes an afterthought. Everyone needs to buy-in to get the desired emotional outcome. Tell the team why it is important, lay out your vision of the activity, give specific details, provide all the necessary tools to make it happen, and make sure the team is interested enough to give it their all. That effort should create the desired positive effect -- to boost morale.

Here are some things to consider when looking to add fun and increase team morale:

- **Make it a Team Effort**: Have the team offer ideas for fun programs. It is not the leader's job to get everyone to enjoy working together. Leaders need to be open-minded, even when they aren't completely sold on what the team came up with. Be a team player and go along with their suggestions.

- **Fun Office Makeover**: Inject brighter colors, beautiful green plants and healthy snacks into an otherwise drab office. Add positive energy.
- **Themed Potluck**: Everyone loves to eat and to share their best recipes. It's a sure way to have tasty fun and introduce new dishes to people.
- **Cooking/ Baking Contests**: Try a fun little competition where you can get to know the cooking talent on your team.
- **Change of Landscape**: Take a walk with your team. Hold a meeting in a park. Have lunch outside on a sunny day. The change of scenery will bring the sunshine back into your office. It's impossible to not feel good after having fresh air fill your lungs and feel the warm sun on your face.
- **Celebrate milestones:** Make a work anniversary a big deal; send flowers with a special note of appreciation. Acknowledge birthdays and don't let personal milestones go by without making them feel like a special occasion. It's one more opportunity to remind people why they love working at your company.
- **Charity or Contribution**: Create ways for your team to connect with your community by supporting those in need. Take suggestions from your employees on what they would like to do, either on their own or as a company, to make the world a better place.
- **Celebrate Holidays with Decorations/ Party**: Around the holidays, join local events or create your own party.
- **Love and Gratitude Letters**: Valentine's Day is a day of love and Thanksgiving a day of gratitude. Both are a great opportunity to send a personalized note or letter of appreciation to someone. Letters give employees an opportunity to see themselves as you see them: valued.
- **Sports Events**: Join a local 5K race, golf tournament, relay race or softball league. Attend a sporting event or sign up as a team sponsor. Whether you're a participant or a spectator, sports can be fun events to do together.
- **Town Square Scavenger Hunt**: Have t-shirts made. Designate teams with colored bandanas. Create teams to work together and

find a list of items around town. Leave clues in envelopes in local businesses. Take photos or videos that can later be shared and posted in the break room for lasting fun. A good scavenger hunt will last a few hours and result in funny stories and solid bonding opportunities.

- **Glass-Blowing or Ceramic Painting Class**: Look for local studios that offer an opportunity for fun and the creation of a treasured gift with lasting memories.

Hiring

The leader's job is to be a talent scout. They must master the ability to match the right talent to the right position within the right team. Skills can be trained, however, happiness and a can-do attitude cannot. Peak performance comes from balancing the level of encouragement/praise and direction/ training each employee needs. Ideally, we are looking to get enthusiastic new hires that receive encouragement, praise and training well and stay on as committed, loyal, competent employees. Empowered employees are inspired, driven and have expertise. They are contributors and partners in executing the business's vision.

Leaders must recognize where each employee is in their professional development cycle in order to effectively coach them. The leader's approach should be highly directive when an employee needs to master skills in order to complete their work; coach-like when needing to offer encouragement and direction when skills are developing; supportive when skills are mastered but the employee is mentally or emotionally rundown; and simply a delegator when an employee needs no support. It is also important to remember that employees are constantly drained by the day-to-day needs of the work environment. They cannot be put on cruise control, but instead need continual nourishment. Ideally, the goal in hiring is to find candidates that can be delegated tasks and can fulfill the duties of their job description with minimal outside support.

To keep employees engaged and challenged, Vicki McManus utilizes a tip that was passed down to her: "If I have an employee who hasn't made a mistake in three weeks, I give him a new task. If people aren't actively making mistakes, they're not growing. It's important to have a culture that says it's okay to make a mistake if you're learning something new. Then people are open to trying new things." Additionally, the same mistake made over and over again is a training opportunity. "Anything that stresses the employee, the customer or the boss is a training opportunity! My core belief is that there are no defects in people, only in systems. Maybe you had a defect in your hiring process or in your training process or in the way you communicated expectations or boundaries." If you've addressed chronic mistakes and provided appropriate training without a change in result, then its time to think about re-assigning the task to someone else. Taking a constructive, praise-oriented approach does not mean you condone sloppy work.

Depending on the size of your organization, having a great HR Administrator is priceless; however, most small businesses don't have that luxury. Hiring, interviewing and "reading" people are skills not all leaders possess. If a person on your team is highly perceptive, picks up on body language and tonality and has a special flair for understanding and engaging people, then include him or her in your hiring process.

Assessment tests can also support leaders in gaining insight into candidates. A few examples include: DISC profile, Highland's Ability Battery, and the Forté Communication Style Reports. These tests help recruit and retain the right people; develop people to improve their skills, improve individual and team performance, and minimize conflict.

- DISC profile is one of the most powerful tools available to companies today because it is simple to interpret. By understanding the predictability of communication and human behavior, one can unlock the true potential and capabilities of the people in the organization, thereby creating compatible teams. The profile uses the basic quadrants of Dominance, Influence, Steadiness, and Conscientiousness. Each person has a unique combination of these 4 DISC Personality Styles.

- Highland's Ability Battery is the gold standard among assessment tools in measuring individual abilities. By means of objective hands-on work samples, it can help leaders understand natural abilities. Knowing the range of a candidate's abilities supports the hiring process. It also helps the candidate better understand how to utilize their unique abilities in life, at work and in relationships with others.

- *Forté Communication Style Reports*[20] gives leaders an individualized and detailed report of "who" the candidate is, how he or she is currently adapting to the environment, and how they are coming across to others. Forté measures communication strengths that reflect decision-making style, people focus, pace, and system/detail focus. There is a full description of each person's primary strength, secondary strength and two sub-strengths.

Leaders can also find out if a candidate is proactive, detail-oriented and fast or slower-paced by setting up simple tests in the interview during the screening process. Here are a few favorites:

1. Crumple up a piece of paper and put in the hallway. Does the candidate stop and pick it up? Do they point it out?

2. Have a pen or piece of paper on the side of the desk near them, and push it onto the floor during the interview. Do they just look at it? McManus says, "If so, they are probably not very organized and not going to care what their workspace looks like. If they say, oh, I'm sorry, you dropped this, then they're conscientious, proactive, and are paying attention to the environment around them."

3. While screening applications, request a one-page cover letter about why they are applying for the job. Or ask a question specific to their resume. Date the back of the application and note how long it takes them to respond. This is a measure of responsiveness and ability to follow detailed instructions.

4. Test applicants by sending an e-mail asking them to call back to schedule an appointment. How well do they organize their thoughts during the conversation? Are they giving necessary information and being concise? Are they pleasant? Are they chatty in the beginning? Again, we are looking for responsiveness within a certain timeframe. McManus states: "Many jobs involve telephone skills. The advent of smart phones and texting has diminished telephone etiquette. Testing for verbal skills in the interview process is essential."

5. Give a tour of the company space at a pace that resembles the energy needed to work in your environment. Does the candidate keep up? If he or she doesn't have the physical stamina to keep up, or if when going down a long hallway they lag behind, then mentally they're not going to be able to keep up in their job.

Another strategy to employ is to ask open-ended questions that evoke stories. Vicki's favorite open-ended interview questions are:

Hire to Inspire

1. **Share with me a time that you went out of your way to make a team member look like a shining star. And you took no credit for it.** It may take a while to think of something, but if the person you're interviewing is passionate, generous and a person of approachability, they don't mind sharing the credit. We are looking for someone who will notice a teammate struggling and help them out, not for their own credit or praise.

2. **Share with me a time when others went out of their way to support you.** The candidate needs to be able to recognize the contributions of their teammates. If they can't think of a time when other people went out of their way to support them, there's a reason and you probably don't want a person who is not able to find the good in their team, on yours.

3. **Share with me a time when you did something outside your comfort zone and participated in an activity that gave you confidence that you didn't know you had.** This answer will show you if the person is willing to try new things. If you are looking for entrepreneurial thinkers, their answer will be telling.

4. **What single task would you consider your most significant accomplishment in your career to date?** Vicki attributes Lou Adler's article in INC magazine (http://www.inc.com/lou-adler/best-interview-question-ever.html) [21] for this question and the follow-up questions. Adler says if you ask this question, then prepare to have a 15-to-20 minute conversation. Then go deeper with follow-up questions like:

- Can you give me a detailed overview of your accomplishment?
- Tell me about the company, your title, your position, your role, and the team involved.
- What were the actual results achieved?
- When did it take place, and how long did the project take?
- Why were you chosen?
- What were the 3 or 4 biggest challenges you faced and how did you deal with them?
- Where did you go the extra mile or take the initiative?
- Walk me through the plan, how you managed it, and its measured success.
- Describe the environment and resources.

- Explain your manager's style and whether you liked it.
- What were the technical skills needed to accomplish the objective, and how were they used?
- What were some of the biggest mistakes you made?
- What aspects of the project did you truly enjoy?
- What aspects did you not especially care about, and how did you handle them?
- Give examples of how you managed and influenced others.
- How did you change and grow as a person?
- What you would do differently if you could do it again?
- What type of formal recognition did you receive?

Your staff never has to feel alone or under-appreciated. Through the VTI portal, all team members proudly view a shared message board where your staff accomplishments and announcements of praise can be posted.

BIOGRAPHY

Vicki McManus is a seriously addicted entrepreneur! Her clinical background as a dental hygienist combined well with continuing education in marketing, finance, and interpersonal communication, to make her one of the leading business development consultants in dentistry.

Over the past nineteen years she has started two award-winning, multi-million dollar companies and lectured throughout the United States, Canada, and Australia. She has shared the stage with Anthony Robbins, Wayne Dyer and other top performance coaches.

She is the co-founder and CEO of Productive Dentist Academy. A 63% growth rate in the previous three years has garnered the company recognition by Inc5000 Fastest Growing Private Companies in 2012, 2013 and 2014.

Ms. McManus was honored to receive the 2013 Silver Stevie Women in Business: Female Entrepreneur of the Year.

She is the collaborative author of *FUNdamentals of Outstanding Dental Teams*, and her latest book *Frustration, The Breakfast of Champions*. She can be reached at info@VickiMcManus.com or 360-588-4705. www.VickiMcManus.com

Chapter 9

Culture of Accountability:
A Conversation with Vicki Suiter

"At the end of the day we are accountable to ourselves –
our success is a result of what we do."
- Catherine Pulsifer

In this chapter, we speak with Vicki Suiter, national speaker, business consultant and coach. She is an expert in creating "Cultures of Accountability," and has done this for hundreds of her client companies. She works directly with leaders to build these cultures, which she believes is a key for building sustainably successful companies.

Suiter's straightforward style helps business owners and leaders maintain clarity and focus on what they need to do to reach their goals. For her, having a Culture of Accountability simply means, "You manage people by results versus tasks, and empower them to take ownership of their jobs versus just being 'helpers.' The result? Employees will be more motivated to meet their objectives, since they know that their work will be measured, monitored, recognized and acknowledged."

Accountability is like having an honor code and a rulebook on how your team members will be accountable to one another. For an honor code to be respected, both you and your employees must be accountable, have a common set of agreements, and have agreed upon a set of standards for how to win the game in the workplace.

Why Build a Culture of Accountability?

Building a culture of accountability means people within your organization hold each other accountable to do what they say they're going to do, when they say they're going do it, and how they say they're going do it. It's a culture where everyone honors their word, treats one another with respect

85

and values the contribution of others. It's an environment that values direct, honest communication. The benefit? Teams build trust, and people feel good about working with you because there is no hidden agenda. They know how to be successful, do what matters and do not think of themselves as pawns. They focus on the important things and are productive.

Employees genuinely want to do their jobs effectively and support the business in meeting its goals. They want to feel as if they're being asked to do something worthwhile that makes a contribution. Interestingly, the more responsibility and ownership you give employees, the more they want to rise to the occasion. A culture that creates this environment builds great morale. A culture of accountability builds better relationships between you and your employees because conversations are more focused and empowering. This also makes work more fun for everyone.

How Do You Create a Culture of Accountability?

You create a culture of accountability by:
- Creating a common set of agreements where both the employees and managers are accountable to each other, and
- Having an agreed-upon set of standards for how you win the game in the workplace.

The key to success is getting buy-in on the agreements. Having leaders and individual employees agree to hold each other accountable to meeting those clearly defined results is the key to having a successful outcome. This means that your employees need a safe environment where they are encouraged to speak up and make suggestions about how to obtain the best results. In our next chapter, Chapter 10, on Participatory Ownership, we will further define the culture in which people who will be affected by a decision are invited to participate in the decision making process.

Ultimately, it begins with leaders being a role model for accountability. Suiter believes that a leader needs to have three character traits in order to bring about a culture of accountability:
1. Courage
2. Ability to manage by results and tell the truth
3. Continually be engaged in an open dialogue

In order for a culture of accountability to truly work, you must keep your agreements, do what you promise by the date promised. Accountability to one another and one's team is far more powerful than accountability to the leader or "boss." Being accountable to each other means that results are accomplished and that everyone on your team is moving in the same direction because everyone knows each other's role.

The next critical piece for building a culture of accountability is setting up employees to win by clearly defining their roles. Job descriptions clearly describe responsibilities, objectives and results. True employee ownership and accountability is achieved with job descriptions, plus an organizational chart that shows everyone's role on the team and within the organization. Let's say you manage a football team in the NFL. How successful would the team be if people didn't know what position they played? What if everyone simply "helped out" wherever they saw a need? It would be pure chaos, with no possibility of winning. Put people in the right positions on your team with an organizational chart, give them guidelines for their position on the team and hold them accountable.

Every successful company has an organizational chart that outlines key roles and responsibilities in a company. This provides clarity and focus about the key role staff plays in the "whole" of the organization and helps them be clear about direct reports and chain of command. A linebacker doesn't go to the kicker for direction; he goes to the coach.

Job descriptions need to be appropriate for the role that each employee holds within the organization. Working on a team has many benefits. Each of us has our own talents that we bring to the team.

How Job Descriptions Can Create a Culture of Accountability

Results-based job descriptions must clearly describe what each person's primary responsibility is and what their primary deliverables are. Employees need to know where to focus their time, not just all the details that need to happen. This allows them to direct their actions and produce key results for their job. In turn, it leads to a higher sense of contribution and greater happiness in their job. Vicki Suiter points out, "Employees have an increased sense of satisfaction because they feel that what they're doing matters. I've gotten this feedback from employees repeatedly over the years "

Employees definitely want to be fairly compensated for the work they do. However, many studies have shown that employees want to make a contribution and feel that what they do is valued and matters. Having a sense of purpose makes coming to work more meaningful and is the way to keep talented people engaged. When employees have clear, results-based job descriptions, they can be given autonomy to fulfill their responsibilities and won't need to be micro-managed.

Autonomy leads to more creativity, innovation, employee engagement, business growth and profitability. Respecting employees' judgments and giving them both accountability and authority within their job description further supports responsibility and motivation.

Another benefit is that people who feel that what they do matters and makes a contribution tend to stay in their job longer. According to Vicki Suiter, "Employees and employers often come back to me after implementing job descriptions in their company and say, 'Wow! I feel like my team is having so much more fun. People are more engaged. People are feeling like they're clear and more confident, and they're willing to take more risks in their job because they know what's expected of them – they know how to win the game!'"

Clearly defined roles with measurable results mean you have a way to measure productivity and achievements. Measuring achievements provides opportunities for you to acknowledge and celebrate your employees' victories and build better relationships with them. Because the job description can stand on its own, the performance appraisal is not personal. This is another benefit of having clear expectations, because only the measurable objective results are evaluated.

To create results-based job descriptions, Vicki Suiter suggests that you get started immediately and involve the employee in writing the job description. Both you and your employee must sign off on the final job description, which becomes an agreement between the two of you. She says, "An interesting thing about human beings is that once we make an agreement about something, our accountability, sense of obligation and commitment go way up."

When the job description is in place, and everyone has signed off and agreed, it now becomes an objective entity that both you and your employee can use to evaluate if things are working or not. This allows you to have more direct, open conversations with your employees, since everyone knows what the criteria for success are for their job. Performance appraisals are more objective, not emotional, conversations, based on stated metrics. There is a lot of work to creating an effective, clearly defined job description, but it is definitely worth it.

Feedback, Performance Appraisals and the Culture of Accountability

Building a culture of accountability includes having open, honest, direct and straightforward communication. Performance appraisals should not be the only time you give feedback; regular and immediate coaching needs to be a part of your culture. When you make an agreement with employees and that agreement is broken, or if somebody is not doing their job, it must be dealt with directly and swiftly. You should not wait and let it build up until you have a "good-enough case."

Vicki Suiter recommends holding performance reviews at least every six months. New employees should have a review at 30 and 90 days from their hire date. She recommends that employees self-evaluate and return the evaluation form prior to the formal review. This allows you time to reflect on how the employee thinks they are doing prior to meeting with them. It's useful to use a rating system on a scale of one-to-six (one being no level of satisfaction, six being exceeding expectations) because you are likely to get a more decisive answer, rather than simply putting a middle number to "play it safe."

Having an employee do a self-review allows for honest feedback and gets employees engaged in evaluating their performance and being accountable. This builds a strong relationship based on trust and allows for direct, honest, straightforward communication. According to Vicki Suiter, "When you make performance review a standard part of your culture, people will tend to work harder and want to be more engaged with you. It will open up more dialogue, which then builds a culture where an employee's level of ownership rises. Leaders move more toward being a coach versus being a manager."

Her core belief is that if you can see it, you can do something about it. When there's clarity about where you are, in contrast to where you want to be, it's much easier to figure out what you need to do next.

Meetings and the Culture of Accountability

Another area where accountability is a necessity is a meeting. There is nothing worse for morale than having team meetings where great brainstorming occurs around certain issues, and none of the action items get implemented. Vicki Suiter recommends having a person at every meeting record what agreements were made, by whom, what was to be done and when it is to be completed. That document is then distributed to everyone in the meeting, and becomes the focal point of the next meeting or any follow- up. This is another opportunity to acknowledge people who accomplish tasks or to give the team progress updates with a new commitment.

Systems for tracking and managing agreements can support everyone in keeping their commitments, maintaining priorities and holding each other responsible. Vicki Suiter cautions you to notice whether you or others are actually making agreements or assumptions that people will do things. If it isn't written down, there isn't an actual traceable agreement. She strongly suggests that at the end of a meeting, in addition to sending out meeting minutes, all the participants go through the list of agreements that were made and confirm that they've made that agreement and by when they would get it done. This way, there's a clear commitment as opposed to an assumption, which can build resentment and anger when there was never an agreement in the first place.

Getting agreement is critically important for building a culture of accountability. Vicki Suiter recommends saying, "This isn't a pressure question. I just want to know when this will get done by, so I know what to expect." It's a simple statement that creates agreement around what, who, and when an action is to occur. It keeps things cleaner, keeps communication more open, eliminates assumptions and avoids having unrealistic expectations.

Hiring and the Culture of Accountability

When hiring a new team member, Suiter encourages leaders to have a written job description before posting an opening, so they are clear about the skills and qualifications needed for the ideal candidate. Post the job description and send a copy of it with the application. She also recommends you always ask for a cover letter and a resume since this will tell you if they read your post completely and followed instructions. You will know if an applicant pays attention to detail, which can be critical, depending on the position.

Suiter suggests that you do phone interviews before in-person interviews, so you can screen whether or not they are a good fit and not waste your time. For the phone interview, she recommends that it be no more than 15-to-30 minutes and that you ask critical questions to identify whether or not this person has actually done this job before.

Hire to Inspire

Always prepare a list of questions for in-person interviews. Make sure they are open-ended questions that require more than a yes-or-no answer, and get the person talking about what he or she has done in previous jobs. Good examples are, "Tell me about a time when you …," or "Tell me what your average day looked like," or, "What would you do in ____ situation?"

Listen for job fit and experience commensurate with your job description and give the candidate time to answer questions thoroughly. Suiter cautions leaders not to spend the interview talking about the company or job – first, let the candidate talk and then, if you think they're a fit, tell them about the company. Have someone with expertise in that area conduct an initial interview. Pay close attention to the candidate's attitude.

When you build a culture that promotes accountability, you don't have to "micromanage" your team. In fact, you can be away from the business more because things will continue to function well without you having to be "in the office" every day. Your employees will have more fun on the job and will enjoy coming to work. The entire atmosphere in your organization will be more positive and energetic.

It will take some work on your part, and you may have to introduce these changes slowly into your organization, but if you persevere, you can build a culture where your employees take responsibility for their actions and produce more consistent results. This is the key for sustainable success for both you and your employees!

VTI's foundation beliefs start with supporting all practices that embrace the Culture of Accountability. Tasks and assignments can be delegated and tracked and progress reports viewed. You can reference the task list and delegate assignments in the portal so management knows exactly when items are completed.

BIOGRAPHY

Vicki Suiter for more than two decades has been helping clients build "cultures of accountability" and sustainably successful companies. Having worked with hundreds of businesses ranging from financial institutions to international leadership development companies, Vicki understands the unique challenges of working *in* a business while simultaneously working *on* it. Her work includes strategic planning, financial projection models/setup, employee accountability structures, as well as feedback systems that get results.

Vicki has presented all over the US and Canada on topics ranging from building stronger profits to changing company culture. To learn more about Vicki Suiter and the services she offers, visit her website at: www.suiterbusinessbuilder.com

---

Start building a Culture of Accountability today! As a special gift to you, Vicki Suiter will send you a special report on **"How to Write Effective Job Descriptions,"** as well as an **"Interview Evaluation Form."** Stop struggling with getting teams aligned and finding the right person for the job by emailing Vicki for these powerful tools today! Vicki@suiterbusinessbuilder.com

---

Chapter 10

Participatory Ownership:
A Conversation with Bernie Stoltz

"I start with the premise that the function of leadership is to produce more leaders, not more followers."
- Ralph Nader

Participatory leadership is when "leaders are leading leaders," which creates partnerships and ownership throughout the organization. In this type of organization, the team is comprised of people who all want the same outcome and will work in concert to achieve a common goal. To develop a culture of participatory ownership, leaders must empower employees to see themselves as being partners versus employees. Partners invest their talents in the organization and support business growth. Partners are passionate and dedicated to realizing the vision of the organization. They create relationships with clients and team members, recognizing the mutual benefit of nurturing these relationships.

In contrast, employees show up for a paycheck and provide a transactional process of trading time for money. These employees will hold back giving their passion and talents to the organization, because they are not fully invested in the outcomes or mission of the organization. They will tend to do the minimal work necessary to keep their job.

What leader doesn't want partners versus employees? Partners take ownership and move in the right direction with the company's goals. Bernie Stoltz is a national speaker and CEO of Fortune Management. He will tell us how to make this model of leadership work, and how it is mutually beneficial to the company and employees. When hiring a team member, Bernie feels it is most important to get to know the candidate's values and rules. He explains how utilizing interview questions like "What is most important to you?" can tell us this.

Participatory Leaders

Great participatory leaders take care of their people by recognizing three important things people want most in today's workforce. First, people want to be paid fairly. Remember, however, "it's not all about the money" and people will not stay just for a good paycheck. Bernie explains, "Finances are how we measure value in the workplace." In his experience, people with good integrity don't want to be overpaid and they certainly don't want to be underpaid; they want to feel they are paid what they're worth, that they are paid in proportion to the value they provide. The best practice is to make sure that there are no limits to what they can earn if they're adding massive value to the workplace. Second, people want to be empowered, need to be able to "own it," to have a voice, and permission to make mistakes. Failure is a crucial and almost always a necessary part of the growth path to success. However, there's more to failure than just learning from your mistakes -- there's owning-up to them, too. Participatory leaders need to state that mistakes are acceptable as long as they are made with the right intentions and in alignment with the company's vision. A great lesson one of Bernie's mentors told him was to try to make small mistakes, not big ones. More importantly, try not to make the same mistake twice. Bernie coaches the mantra, "FFF -- let them fall, forward, fast" to empower teams. "FFF" means not restricting people's ability to learn or to fear making mistakes. The greatest lessons in life come from the personal experience of making mistakes and correcting them. It's critical that leaders never fault their people for making mistakes that have been made with the right intentions. Third, people want purpose and to believe that they matter. Being part of a vision gives people a "power of purpose" to provide meaningful work. Participatory leaders understand the importance of "power of purpose" in having a vision people believe in. People want to believe they have a voice and a role in creating the vision, which gives them their purpose.

Must-have characteristics and actions of the participatory leader include:

Strong core values that exude integrity, happiness, abundance and gratitude. Leaders with strong core values become beloved through exhibiting moral character in their everyday actions that protect the team culture.

- Courage- Courageous leaders recognize fear as "False Evidence that Appears Real." John Wayne summed it up perfectly when he said, "Courage is being scared as hell, but saddling up anyway."
- Optimism- Unlocking people's potential is the greatest gift leaders

have to give. Optimistic leaders turn dreams into reality, by seeing things and people as better than they are. A leader must be a person who takes the high road at all times. This requires not letting their feelings or others dictate their emotions. "Nothing in life has any meaning except the meaning you give it." – Anthony Robbins

- <u>Do their homework</u>- Leaders must work on their business and be proactive in doing knowledge work, which leads to project work, versus being reactive and only doing work as it appears. Work as it appears is the least profitable because it is not as efficient or as well-thought-out. To maximize profitability and be effective, leaders must do knowledge work. Leaders create their own LUCK, "Labor Under Correct Knowledge." Successful leaders believe in the power of action as the cause of success and that opportunity is everywhere, so they have to be prepared.

- <u>Learn to work well with a team</u>- The best leaders let go of ego and seek to hire people smarter than they are. Leaders can be in a partnership with their team when they release their ego and embrace the success of the team. To release egos, leaders must accept that they are only limited by their abilities and that they don't have all the answers. Letting go of ego means not having to be right, choosing to be effective and choosing to be in relationships. Further transformation occurs when leaders recognize they do not need to be better than others; they just need to be better than they were before.

- <u>Influential</u>- Communication is the key to success for every person in the organization. However, beyond being a good communicator leaders need to be great influencers. Nothing happens until someone sells someone else. The best influencers ask questions and transfer ownership to transform a want into a need. "Leadership is the art of getting someone else to do something you want done because he wants to do it." —General Dwight D. Eisenhower

- <u>Make decisions</u>- Leaders need to make decisions so that the organization can do the right thing at the right time. Perfection paralysis will cripple growth and close doors to opportunity. Whether leaders make winning decisions or learning decisions, they will find more opportunities open up for them.

Additionally, great leaders will continually self-evaluate if they're "walking their talk." Reflecting introspectively, leaders can learn a lot by putting themselves on the other side of the equation. Bernie Stoltz suggests leaders ask themselves, "If I wasn't the leader here, would this still be a really cool company for me to work at? Could I survive here? Could I not only survive, but flourish under my own regime?" Beloved leaders won't ask more of their people than they are willing to contribute themselves, and don't have double standards.

Culture of Participatory Ownership

Following the principles of participatory ownership means creating a culture whereby every person on the team feels he or she is a partner operating a "business within a business." Partners have the ability to control their earning potential to some degree. The creation of this culture starts with the leader leading versus managing, and instilling a culture of proactivity versus reactivity. Managing has an internal focus that remains in a short-range problem-solving mode, which will be an on-going resource allocation process, a never-ending loop. Leading has an external focus that provides a long-range visionary process and focuses on people, communication and innovation. Leading is all about the power of questions and seeing the future before it happens. Influential leaders create a compelling future for their partners to engage and embrace.

Most leaders would agree the ultimate outcome of leadership is to provide the least management intervention. Participatory leadership creates sustainable growth for the organization by providing peak performers who continue to gift their talents freely. A peak performer is someone who knows exactly how to do their job and is self-motivated to achieve results. They don't need management or direction to complete their job. In fact, they don't need a lot of coaching inspiration because they get that from within. The vision and mission inspires them to achieve.

A participatory ownership culture has energy that is much more fulfilling for all involved. A proactive organization is created by leading rather than managing. Organizational growth occurs because people are empowered to grow and innovate. This increases organizational bandwidth exponentially, because the more people are empowered to own individual parts, the more the organization can achieve as a whole. People will tend to show up the way leaders expect them to. Meaning, if the leadership expects more from every single person, then people will meet those expectations.

Bernie Stoltz reminds us, "You get what you ask for in life." A proactive culture leads by example and assures that everyone within the organization knows that their leadership is their biggest fan and their biggest advocate. Participatory leaders recognize they are in the business of helping every person in their organization to be able to achieve their dreams. In other words, the organization cannot be just for profit or just for ownership and investors to achieve their dreams. The participatory ownership culture happens when everybody knows they can all fulfill their dreams by creating value within the organization. 1:1 meetings are the best way for leaders to find out what their people want to achieve. This is when leadership sits down individually with every person to find out what his or her hopes, dreams, and aspirations are, and sets up a vision for what their life will look like in one, two, five, ten years. When leaders actively invest the time to be in 1:1 meetings and ask these questions of the people on their team, it shows they care about individual success. This is when participatory ownership flourishes and partnerships form.

Bernie Stoltz has grown his organization Fortune Management through the philosophy of participatory ownership; he coaches other businesses to do the same. He decided nearly twenty years ago that he never again wanted to be in management; instead, he wanted to lead people to their dreams. Fortune Management is an organization that teaches leadership, not management. The corporate mission is to help people turn their dreams into realities. Bernie Stoltz hires people whose personal vision includes adding value to other people's lives. His people make their own hours, can work virtually, get paid in proportion to the value they provide, and are in a position to do purposeful work to make a difference in their clients' lives. Every person within Fortune Management is a business within a business.

"There's not one person within Fortune who has a cap on what their earning potentials are. They know that they've got to own their successes, and their failures too." Fortune extends these teachings to their client base as well. The Fortune mantra is, "If we teach it, we do it, and if we don't do it, we don't teach it." First, Fortune establishes within the client's businesses a win-win bonus system, not because it's about the money but because it's a rallying point for the execution of the business. Second, Fortune insists on group masterminding and establishing monitoring systems to provide focus, direction and a measurement of success. Group masterminding allows for greater success by giving leaders perspective and studying obstacles from all levels within their organization. Group masterminding also establishes better buy-in, because when more people have been part of the process, they are more likely to own it. This allows people to dream big and to bring their own individual personalities in to shine.

These great thoughts and ideas add a blended personality to the organization and distinguish it as unique, creative and innovative. In this culture, everyone knows they have freedom of speech and are encouraged to share their ideas in the masterminding, which also establishes the opportunity for team agreements to be followed. Monitoring systems are necessary to define success and identify what winning looks like. Success can only occur if everyone knows where and how to get to the finish line. Additionally, everyone must know his or her role in the race and properly hand off the baton so the team can cross the finish line.

To establish a culture of participatory ownership, make sure everyone knows that the organization can be their vehicle to get everything they want, not just in their professional life, but in their personal endeavors as well. Do this by asking great questions of every person on the team and take a real interest in each person's professional goals and personal dreams. To maximize human capital, leaders need to accomplish five steps:

Proper team selection is critical- Select the right people based on their beliefs, values, and attitudes.

Invest in your people with the right training- They need to know how to play the game. Leaders need to give them the necessary skill sets to accomplish their jobs and to have continual growth.

Inspire and motivate them- Leaders must coach their team through asking questions.

Monitor the results that everyone on the team is bringing- Participatory-driven teams do pay attention to the results.

Celebrate successes and thank people- Beyond bonuses, leaders need to have reward systems to make sure that they know how much you appreciate them.

Hiring and Interview Questions

> *"A great person attracts great people and knows how to hold them together."*
> - Johann Wolfgang Von Goethe

Proper team selection involves matching shared core beliefs, values, attitudes and personal visions with those the organization needs to fill the position. You find out through asking great questions in the interview process:

- What's most important to you in your life? In a career? In being on a team? Helping people? Listen closely for the candidate's core values to see if they match the organization's values.
- Follow the values questions with the rules questions.
- What would have to happen for you to feel like this is an incredible career?
- What would have to happen for you to feel like you're doing purposeful work here?
- What would have to happen for you to feel like you're on the same page with leadership on the vision?
- What would have to happen for you to feel like the vision is something you're really energized and excited and passionate about?
- Where do you want to be a year from now in your career? In two years? In five years?
- Why do you want to be part of this team?
- What do you believe about the world? About people? About a career?

The final question will reveal if they are proactive or reactive. A reactive person is going to think it's okay to blame other people. They live their life being a victim and believing in scarcity. Reactive people are good at discovering problems, not solutions. Proactive people are optimistic and see problems as opportunities. They are problem-solvers.

Your team can participate in and contribute to the practice and have skin in the game through rewards-based incentives. Allow your employees to step up their game and become leaders. Your VTI portal teaches them, and also provides them a place to get organized, study and teach. With a project manager tool, shared calendar task tools and trackers, you and your team are empowered to keep an eye on the ball and hit those business targets out of the park.

BIOGRAPHY

Bernie Stoltz- In early 1990, Bernie Stoltz's infectious enthusiasm and simple-to-implement business strategies caught the eye of Anthony Robbins, world-famous personal achievement coach and author. Since then, Bernie has conducted hundreds of training programs across the globe to help thousands of dentists become their professional and personal best.

Bernie brings over 20 years of business leadership to dentistry and was the founder of five successful companies before founding Fortune Management of California, Inc. He works with some of the top practices in the country and provides the competitive edge that practices need to succeed today.

A regular contributor to dental publications, Bernie has taught practice management at the UCSF School of Dentistry and at the acclaimed P.A.C.~ live. Bernie has dedicated his life to achievement in the areas of marketing, public relations, advertising and business management.

Bernie is a no-nonsense speaker who packs his programs with relevant information. He is known for presenting practical solutions for complex issues that practices face today. Participants will have an outstanding experience and leave with practical information that will make a difference in their business and their personal lives.

Chapter 11

Unstoppable Teams Go Further

By Jennifer Chevalier

There is no task more challenging or rewarding than building a powerful organization. Leading a successful team creates a great environment, happy workers, and, best of all – unstoppable results.

Knowing your Team

When assembling a team, the leader requires a keen understanding of his or her people. They must know each individual's strengths, what excites them, and where they are most powerfully utilized. You can build an unstoppable team if you really know all your great players and place them in the right positions.

The first aspect of knowing your team is knowing yourself. This will enable you to drive yourself and your team to extraordinary achievement. Tools such as DISC or Myers-Briggs will allow you to assess yourself and your behavior in order to provide insight into the real you. The secret to these tests is to see them as a temporary reflection of your personality at any given moment. They do not have to reflect a permanent state and, if used correctly, you should be able to create a more balanced self by focusing on the weaknesses you wish to strengthen. Because you will be in a position to anticipate your behaviors and actions in various situations, you can then create strategies that allow you to overcome and manage behaviors that get in the way of being an effective leader.

A *Harvard Business Review* article written by Daniel Goleman states, "Effective leaders are alike in one crucial way: They all have a high degree of emotional intelligence.[22]" Goleman defines emotional intelligence as comprised of five components: self-awareness, self-regulation, motivation, empathy and social skill.

The knowledge of emotional intelligence is basic for a successful leader. Specific skills have to do with self-knowledge, the ability to read individuals and groups, and the ability to communicate with and influence others. People who improve in these areas tend to be effective in their personal relationships as well as in business interactions, organizational challenges, collaboration, and leadership. When these skills are applied at work, a person becomes a better leader and a more desirable employee.

Though you may be in charge, those who work for you may not appreciate how you work. You may have good intentions, but make sure you hold yourself accountable to course-correct and modify your approach, if necessary, to assure that you're leading from a position of strength and respect.

Just as you hold yourself accountable for your actions to assure you maximize your performance and results, you must also take the time to get to know your team. Part of being an exceptional leader means understanding the needs of your team, embracing their differences and helping your colleagues experience their significance. In this case, gathering intelligence means learning what defines the strengths and capabilities of your team, the real assets that each member brings to the table, and those assets yet to be developed. Fully knowing your team means that you have invested the time to understand how they are wired and what is required to motivate them to excel.

Clearly Define Roles and Responsibilities

Once you have done your entire discovery in knowing and understanding your team, you can more effectively define their roles and responsibilities. In Chapter Six, Vicki Suiter explains the critical piece for building a culture of accountability, writing job descriptions that describe responsibilities, objectives and results. Creating results-based job descriptions is different from what most managers are used to.

An ordinary job description can often be confused for a task list or a checklist. An effective job description keeps the focus on the purpose of the employee and what the results should be when the job is executed correctly. I like to say, good job descriptions eliminate the gray area between employee and employer. If a role has been clearly defined and agreed-upon, the risk for misunderstanding is reduced. People know where they need to be and what is expected of them. By clearly defining employee roles from the start, not only do we target and hire the best, most qualified candidates, but we also ensure their continued success by informing them exactly how that success will be determined and measured.

With the role of each individual in the organization defined, you can also create an organization chart. This is a tool that helps to define the inter-relationships among all departments, divisions, teams and people. It defines reporting structures and lines of authority and responsibility, providing a picture of how the organization functions.

Training and Development

What is training? For the purpose of this chapter, training is: a) Transferring information and knowledge to employees, and b) Translating that information and knowledge into practice, with a view to enhancing the organization's effectiveness and productivity.

Not investing time and money into a company's training and development is the biggest mistake any organization can make. Well-trained employees are essential to the success of your business and unfortunately, this is the most neglected part in a small-to-mid-size organization. A lack of training can reduce motivation levels, business efficiencies and, most detrimentally, result in staff turnover.

Staff turnover is one of the highest cost factors to a small business, costing on average 100-to-125 percent of an employee's annual salary in lost productivity, hiring costs and new hire training. One of the most important benefits of training for an organization is that it provides skills inside the organization, which reduces the overall cost of operations. Quality is one of the key features required for the long-term survival of an organization.

Understanding the cost of staff turnover in a small-to-mid-size business was one of the major motivations for creating Virtual Training Innovations. When we evaluated the intrinsic costs of losing and replacing an employee, it was clear that smaller organizations were neglecting this aspect. It is much more cost-effective to invest in your current employees than to re-start the process by replacing them. We also discovered that employee retention had a direct effect on customer satisfaction. Better training can provide a competitive advantage over other companies.

Proactive Feedback

Feedback is the key to assuring that any team is staying on track, and more importantly, that it is improving. Feedback should be proactive and constant. Many leaders wait until a problem occurs before they give feedback.

Feedback in its purest form is quality communication. As a leader, feedback should be considered part of one's natural dialogue and should be authentic and positively impactful. Allow proactive feedback to serve as your team's greatest enabler for continuous improvement.

In Chapter Seven, Shannon Richkowski, RDH, speaks to one of my favorite topics, C.A.N.I.®. Constant and Never-ending Improvement is one of the most powerful mottos a business can adopt. When we come from a place of knowing things can always be improved, it helps us emotionally detach from needing to be right. If you want to be more successful, you need to learn to ask yourself, "How can I make this better? How can I do it more efficiently, more profitably?" Strong leaders often think they need to have all the right answers, when really they just need to ask the right questions.

In today's world, a certain amount of improvement is necessary just to keep up with the rapid pace of change. In many ways, improving is necessary to survival. But to thrive, a more dedicated approach to improvement comes in small increments. Whenever we set out to improve our skills, change our behavior or better our business, beginning in small, manageable steps gives us a greater chance of long-term success.

Acknowledge and Reward

People love recognition, but are most appreciative of respect. Take the time to give your teammates the accolades they have earned and deserved. I have seen too many leaders take performance for granted because they don't believe that someone should be rewarded for "doing their job." When people are acknowledged, their work brings them greater satisfaction and they become more purposeful. If employees feel that they are serving a useful purpose, they are much more likely to stay in their current job.

A common complaint from employees in small-to-mid-size organizations is that they feel burned out, and a common symptom of that is feeling unappreciated. One of the best ways to address burnout and retain employees is to ensure that they feel appreciated for their work. People want to make a difference, so be a thoughtful leader and reassure your team that you are paying attention to their efforts. Being genuine in your recognition and respect goes a long way toward building loyalty and trust.

There are many ways to reward people for their quality of the work in the workplace -- through money, benefits, time off from work, acknowledgment for work well done, affiliation with coworkers or a sense of accomplishment from finishing a major task.

Rewards should support behaviors directly aligned with accomplishing strategic goals. This principle may seem so obvious as to sound trite. However, the goal of carefully tying employees' behaviors to strategic goals has only become important over the past decade or so. Recently, the term "performance" is being used to designate behaviors that really contribute to the "bottom line." An employee can be working as hard as anyone else, but if his/her behaviors are not tied directly to achieving strategic goals, then the employee might only be doing busywork.

When rewarding your team, clearly associate the reward to accomplishments. Imagine if someone said "Thank you" but did not say what for. One of the purposes of a reward is to reinforce the positive behaviors that earned the reward. If employees understand what behaviors they are being rewarded for, they are more likely to repeat them.

Know When to Stop and Celebrate Success

Recognizing achievements and milestones boosts pride, camaraderie, and leadership credibility. At a time when there is so much uncertainty, you must take the time to celebrate success. This goes beyond acknowledgments. It is about taking a step back and reflecting on what people have accomplished and learned throughout the journey.

In today's fast-paced, rapidly changing world of work, people are not taking enough time to understand why they are successful and how their success positively impacts those around them. Celebrating accomplishments in the workplace can have a major impact on successes in the organization. Simply put, when employees see that the company rewards and celebrates good work, each person is motivated. This results in a team that works much harder to achieve, and encourages success in future endeavors.

Creating an unstoppable team takes time. It is a process with many steps, not one of which can be skipped. Great teams and great cultures are not born overnight, but the decision to create them is. So commit today to start creating the unstoppable team that will bring unstoppable results tomorrow.

Hire to Inspire

Professional team-building has never been easier. Use your VTI portal and unleash the power of human performance. A great place to effectively train your team with duplicatable systems, customized to your practice. Save time and money, invest in your people, teach them to "fish" and they will add tremendous value to your practice investment. VTI helps you build leaders among leaders for an unstoppable team.

BIOGRAPHY

Jennifer L. Chevalier is the CEO and Co-founder of Virtual Training Innovation. Growing up in the world of practice management and personal development, Jennifer got a strong understanding of what it takes to be successful in the world at a very young age. In high school, Jennifer was drawn towards dentistry and even considered the path towards dental school. She was able to work in some of the most elite dental practices in the Bay Area, learning how the best practices ran their businesses. She was able to work in almost every front and back office position learning them thoroughly. During this time Jennifer discovered her passion for business and how creating successful private practices led to improving the standards of healthcare.

After receiving her Bachelor's degree in Business Administration with an emphasis on Marketing and a minor in Communications from San Jose State University, Jennifer started working as a marketing consultant to many private practices in healthcare. With her extensive knowledge in practice management she knew that all the marketing in the world would not help private practices that did not have the right systems in place. One of the systems that she discovered was broken in many offices was training. One of her clients, Yolanda Mangrum, DDS had started Jennifer on a project for her practices called her team "intranet" site. After months of investigation and thought out ideas, Jennifer and Yolanda decided this was an idea worth venturing into and a product all private practices needed. Jennifer knows Virtual Training will be one of the greatest contributions she could give to healthcare and businesses worldwide.

Conclusion

Success is a Journey, not a Destination

By Yolanda Mangrum, DDS

> *"Life is a journey, not a destination."*
> - Ralph Waldo Emerson

Too often, we leaders get so caught up in being successful, achieving goals, creating our vision, and problem-solving, we can forget to enjoy the moment and we ignore our blessings. So I write these final thoughts for the book as a reminder to myself, as much as to anyone else. To remember making every moment count means scheduling some downtime to pause, think about our accomplishments, and feel grateful. That is when we can find clarity to see the opportunities surrounding us. Absolutely continue to seize the day, but don't lose track of the moments, especially those that deserve celebrating. The truth is, no matter how much we achieve, accomplish, and acquire in life, there is always something more to be had. We will never "reach" that absolutely final destination or achieve all of our goals. Honestly, knowing that our successes and failures are infinite is what makes life that much more interesting and fun.

Admittedly, it's so easy to get out of balance because things just don't go perfectly as planned. Our focus too often is on gearing up for the next big challenge or analyzing what didn't go according to plan instead of taking the time to celebrating our wins. Remind yourself and your team that the key to obtaining happiness is to focus on enjoying the journey, taking the time to "smell the roses," and focusing on what's really important in life. This doesn't mean that we have to give up on dreaming big or setting big goals. It's good to be ambitious; it's great to want to accomplish the seemingly impossible, but just remember to push the pause button every now and then to celebrate the wins and count your blessings. Happiness comes from living in the present and doing more of what gives you joy. How will you know what really makes you happy unless you take time to revel in your reactions? Only you have the power to control your emotions, so turn up the volume on the happy ones and turn down the volume on the negative ones. Be kind to yourself. We have our greatest growth from our failures, so learn from your mistakes and move forward.

Finally, do more of what makes you feel happy and eliminate what makes you sad. "Live wise, love well, serve greatly" is a quote from Robin Sharma in his book *The Saint, the Surfer, and the CEO*[23]. This is my daily reminder to evaluate how I am living my life.

It is my hope that *Hire to Inspire* will serve you well on your own journey.

Through developing your practice systems, growing your team, and expanding your services, you'll find that your VTI portal grows with you. As you store new technology, team members, and systems, the portal will prove to be an excellent vehicle for supporting your practice. The value of your practice will be exponentially increased. Reliable, duplicatable systems…this will be your road map on your journey toward professional success.

BIOGRAPHY

Yolanda Mangrum, DDS, is the COO and Co-Founder of Virtual Training Innovations. She has been a practicing dentist since 1997 and owner of her practice since 1999. The need to create Virtual Training Innovation came about because, "Keeping my team on track with training, culture, goals and protocols has seemed like a never-ending, frustrating task. I needed to create a way to stop this cycle and win." Throughout her practicing years, she has created protocols to achieve repeatable systems and lay the groundwork for inspiring individual growth.

Dr. Mangrum began her dental career in 1989 when she received on-the-job training to become a licensed Registered Dental Assistant. While working as a dental assistant, she completed her Bachelor's in Biology at University of California Riverside, and also completed Riverside City College's Dental Laboratory Technician Certificate.

At University of California San Francisco, School of Dentistry, she was an active student leader and student teacher. After graduation, she received a faculty position as Assistant Clinical Professor. Teaching and learning have remained passions for Dr. Mangrum. She began her service in organized dentistry in 1994, and held local and state positions, culminating in President of the California Academy of General Dentistry in 2008. In 2001, she earned her Fellowship in AGD and received the prestigious Award of Masters in AGD in 2007.

Dr. Mangrum opened her first dental practice in 1999 in Sonoma from scratch, one patient at a time. Ten years later, she purchased her second practice, Petaluma Dental Group. She has built a team of dedicated health care professionals dedicated to C.A.N.I. ® (Constant and Never-Ending Improvement). Being a strong leader is important to her and she enjoys unlocking greatness in every employee. It is her belief that individuals have limitless potential for growth.

Appendices

Tests, Assessments, and Worksheets

Each test in the following pages is available in a printable form at:

http://bit.ly/hiretoinspire

Participatory Leadership Test

The goal is to have leaders leading leaders in our organization of happy people who act as partners committed to creating our vision while maintaining our core values and our culture.

This leadership test can be a self-test or a team assessment of an individual.

Leader's Name: _____   Date: _____

The leader (check one of the three)	Always	Mostly	Sometimes	Rarely
Has impeccable direct communication with customers, team and self. Utilizes communication skills that control their emotions, and expresses themselves professionally.				
Leads by example the behaviors they expect in their team and walk their talk; remains in "It's Showtime" mode in front of their team.				
Is influential, enthusiastically inspiring hope, and has a clear vision.				
Does what they say they're going to do, maintaining commitments with high integrity and trustworthiness.				
Exhibits an optimistic outlook, turns dreams into reality by seeing possibilities in both team and organization.				
Is solution-oriented and results-driven.				
Shows compassion and appreciation regularly to their team. Provides open and honest feedback immediately, with corrective action, so team knows what direction to head.				
Is open to change and shows flexibility in their approach.				

Hire to Inspire

The leader (check one of the three)	Always	Mostly	Sometimes	Rarely
Maintains ownership for their decisions and all the results, while giving the appropriate credit to the team for their successes.				
Delegates appropriately and works well in a team. Has no ego problem, accepting that they don't always have the answers.				
Decisive in making the right decision at the right time.				
Takes initiative and follows through with implementation.				
Courageously holds the line, protecting the organization's culture and core values.				
Exemplifies integrity and has strong personal core values.				
Consistently does their homework and is prepared for surprises.				
"Walks the floor," interacting with their team, takes the pulse of the organization and assesses status and needs of their team.				
Celebrates both individuals' and organization's successes often.				

Organization Culture Test

The goal is to have leaders leading leaders in our organization of happy people who act as partners committed to creating our vision while maintaining our core values and our culture.

This test is for individuals to assess participatory ownership and team culture anonymously.

Date: _____

I feel the organization (check one of the 3)	Always	Mostly	Sometimes	Rarely
Has impeccable direct communication with customers, team and self-talk. Utilizes communication tools that control their emotions and expresses themselves professionally.				
Operates in "It's Showtime" mode in front of our customers and team.				
Remains enthusiastic, focused, and driving toward our vision.				
Does what we say we are going to do, maintaining our commitments with high integrity and trustworthiness.				
Exhibits an optimistic outlook toward turning dreams into reality by seeing possibilities in team members and in the organization.				
Is solution-oriented and results-driven.				
Shows compassion and appreciation to others. Provides immediate open and honest feedback.				
Is open to change and flexible in approach.				
Maintains ownership for our actions and gives the appropriate credit to individuals for our successes.				

Hire to Inspire

I feel the organization (check one of the 3)	Always	Mostly	Sometimes	Rarely
Works well as a team. Lets go of ego, accepting that we don't have all the answers all the time.				
Provides purposeful work that we can all be proud of.				
Takes initiative and follows through with implementation.				
Courageously holds the line, protecting our organization's culture and core values.				
Exemplifies integrity, has strong core values and makes the right decisions at the right time.				
Consistently does homework and is prepared for the unexpected.				
Has engaging and productive team meetings where everyone participates openly and feels heard.				
Celebrates both individual and organizational successes.				
Encourages personal and professional growth, recognizing that this is how the organization thrives.				

A, B or C-Level Employee Test

First, let's always remember that there is no such thing as a perfect employee, or a perfect human being, for that matter. We all have our strengths and weaknesses. It is important to come from the belief that people generally have good intentions and to question only behaviors, not intentions. Employees are not forever tagged as A-, B-, or C-level employees. The purpose of this test is to inspire and direct behaviors to maintain A-level employees.

This test can be a self-test or can be scored by the leader or team for direct feedback.

Employee name: _____ Date: _____

	A-Level Employee	B-Level Employee	C-Level Employee	Team Member Score A, AB, B, BC, or C
Contribution	Self-motivated and self-initiated, internally motivated or only slightly motivated by external factors, mostly self-driven.	Does what is asked, maybe even more, is sometimes self-motivated and is driven by external factors.	Does the minimum to not get fired.	
Makes decisions	Makes the right decision at the right time.	Makes the right decision, but not always in the right timing.	May or may not make the right decision, often needs to be told what to do.	
Company partner versus employee Often says	Partner, takes personal ownership. "We can," "I will," "How can I help?"	Wants to do a good job. "Yes, but...."	Works only for the paycheck. "We can't," "I can't."	
Embraces the company vision	Sees the company vision as his or her own personal mission.	Knows the vision and does his or her best to meet the expectations of their job duties, but may not fully understand how their job relates to company mission.	Not aware of what the vision is, or knows, but doesn't relate to it personally.	
Problem-solving	Excellent problem-solvers, always offers solutions to problems and is willing to do whatever it takes to solve it.	Brings problems to leader that need attention and may suggest solutions, but is not necessarily committed to doing whatever it takes. That's the leader's responsibility.	Doesn't acknowledge there is a problem unless he is personally affected. Sees it as the leader's job to fix.	

Hire to Inspire

	A-Level Employee	B-Level Employee	C-Level Employee	Team Member Score A, AB, B, BC, or C
Prioritizing work	Prioritize their work according to the company vision and mission.	Understands their job and prioritizes within their job duties, but may not always be serving the company vision and mission.	May do what is asked of them, but doesn't necessarily know what to do without being told.	
Taking initiative	Brings new ideas and is committed to initiate them.	Often initiates something that keeps them from doing their job effectively.	No initiative.	
Volunteers to support co-workers, company and team	Eagerly volunteers without being asked.	Volunteers when asked or is personaly invested.	Does not volunteer to do more than it takes to keep their job.	
Ownership	Takes ownership for their actions and team accountability without singling out who's at fault. Will look for ways to take on more responsibility.	Generally takes ownership of his actions, but will not necessarily take team ownership. May point out team member deficiencies to make themselves look better.	No ownership, deflects responsi-bility for their actions. Is the first to point fingers at others when they mistakes.	
Technical skills	Exceptionally skilled, looks for ways to continually improve their skills, and is willing to share what they know to better the team and the company.	Good or even great skills. Doesn't share with team, either because he is not committed enough to the company in a partnership or is afraid of potential competition.	Minimally skilled, neither motivated to improve nor willing to share their knowledge.	
Communication skills	Impeccable direct communication with customers, team and self. Knows how to control his emotions and expresses himself professionally.	Good customer communication, but often has indirect communication within team and is insecure at times, leading to poor self-communication and emotional control.	Frequently gossips, regularly partici-pates in indirect communication and is often emotionally out of control.	

A-level teams will support B-level employees to rise to A-level and will encourage C-levels to find their happy place on another team or in a different position.

117

1 to 1 Growth Conference Pre-Meeting Survey
(to be completed and turned in at least one week prior to meeting date)

Name: _____ 1:1 Date/time: _____ Next Follow-up 1:1 Date: _____

What projects are you currently working on? 1. 2. 3.	What isn't working right yet in our organization or with your projects? 1. 2. 3.
What changes could we make in your job position so that you are more effective, more productive?	What support or training do you need from your team or leadership?
What's the most important professional decision you're facing. What's keeping you from making it?	What threats or weaknesses do you see in see in our company? What should we doing that we're not doing?
What do you see in your future that you would like to do that you're not currently doing? What training do you think you would need to do that?	List personal or professional plan commitments for this year. How are you progressing to reach them? Financial: Relationships: Health: Family: Personally: Other:

What progress have you made on your previous commitments from the last 1:1?

What single thing could you do this month bring the most value to our company?	What is the most important thing we should to be discussing/dialoging about at this 1:1?

Hire to Inspire

Happiness Assessment

Recognizing happiness is definitely an individual choice, and appreciation for what we have is critical to maintaining happiness. Our organization strives to be surrounded by happy people who act as partners committed to creating our vision while maintaining our core values and culture. Open communication about job satisfaction is one way we can show our commitment to achieving our mission.

This assessment is to determine if the employee's needs are being met.

Name: _____   Date: _____

I would like (check one of the three)

	More	Less	Am Happy
Positive feedback, praise, and acknowledgment for my work			
Respect for my individual and team contributions			
Defined goals and objectives			
Clarification about how my job affects the company vision			
Advanced training			
Opportunities to lead our team			
Opportunities for decision making			
Responsibility			
Workload			
Supervision			
A structured work environment			
More team meetings			
Freedom of expression			
Opportunities for contribution			
Purposeful work			
Safety in my work environment			
Confidence in my work			

Endnotes/Recommended Reading

1. Ford, Henry. http://www.brainyquote.com/quotes/authors/h/henry_ford.html
2. Campbell, Steven. *Making Your Mind Magnificent: Flourishing At Any Age,* 1st Edition. (Aviva Publishing, 2010)
3. Collins, Jim. *Good to Great* (Harper Business, 2001)
4. *State of the American Workplace: Employee Engagement Insights for U.S. Business Leaders* (2013) http://www.gallup.com/strategicconsulting/163007/state-american-workplace.aspx
5. Gaille, Brandon. *17 Employee Motivation Statistics and Trends,* (2013)http://brandongaille.com/17-employee-motivation-statistics-and-trends/
6. Robbins, Anthony. *Awaken the Giant Within* (Summit Books, 1991)
7. Wakeman, Cy. *Reality Based Leadership: Ditch the Drama, Restore Sanity to the Workplace, and Turn Excuses into Results* (Jossey-Bass 2010)
8. Hsieh, Tony. *Delivering Happiness: A Path to Profits, Passion, and Purpose* (Business Plus, 2010)
9. The Chilling Letter General Eisenhower Drafted In Case The Nazis Won On D-Day more: http://www.businessinsider.com/d-day-in-case-of-failure-letter-by-general-eisenhower-2012-6#ixzz3B27gOQQh
10. Goldsmith, Marshall. *What Got You Here Won't Get You There: How Successful People Get More Success* (Hyperion 2007)
11. Sinek, Simon. *Start with why: How Great Leaders Inspire Everyone to Take Action* (Penguin Group 201)
12. Lencioni, Patrick. *Five Dysfunctions of a Team* (Jossey-Bass, 2002)
13. Lily, Stephen. Director of the Movie "Perfect Effort"[13], (2007)
14. Chapman, Gary & White, Paul W. *The 5 Languages of Appreciation in the Workplace (*Moody Publishers, 2012)
15. Ball, William. *A Sense Of Direction: Some Observations on the Art of Directing,* (2003)

16. Robbins, Anthony. *Ultimated Power: The New Power of Personal Achievement* (Free Press 2003)

17. McManus, Vicki, RDH, *Fundamentals of Outstanding Dental Teams* (James & Brookfield Publishers, 1998)

18. McManus, Vicki RDH. *Frustration, the Breakfast of Champions,* (2014)

19. Lundin, Stephen PhD, Paul, Harry and Christensen, John. *Fish!: A Remarkable Way to Boost Morale And Improve Results* (Many Rivers Press, 1996)

20. *Forté Communication Style Reports*- http://www.theforteinstitute. com

21. Adler, Lou. *The Only Interview Question That Matters* (INC magazine, 2014) (http://www.inc.com/lou-adler/best-interview-question-ever.html)

22. Goleman, Daniel. *What makes a good leader?* (Harvard Business Review, 2004)

23. Sharma, Robin. *The Saint, the Surfer, the CEO* (Hay House, 2003)

24. Banks, Lydia. *Motivation in the Workplace: Inspiring Your Employees* (American Media Publishing1997)

25. Cottrell, David. *The Magic Question: A Simple Question Every Leader Dreams of Answering* (Conner Stone Leadership Institute, 2012)

26. Deporter, Bobbi, *The 8 Keys of Excellence: Principles to Live By* (Learning Forum Publications, 2010)

27. Maxwell, John, *Developing the Leaders Around You: How to Help Others Reach Their Full Potential* (Injoy, 1995)

28. Quick, Thomas. *Inspiring People at Work: How to Make Participative Management Work For You* (Executive Enterprises Publication Co., Inc 1986)

29. Hubbard, Elbert, *Message to Gracia* (Roycrofters, 1916)

Made in the USA
San Bernardino, CA
30 April 2015